IS IRISH CATHOLICISM DYING?

Is Irish Catholicism Dying?

Liberating an Imprisoned Church

PEADAR KIRBY

Christian Classics, Inc.
Post Office Box 30
Westminster, Maryland 21157
1984

American edition printed with permission from The Mercier
Press Limited, 4 Bridge Street, Cork, Ireland

ISBN: 0-87061-112-7
Printed in the U.S.A.

To Toni, my life's companion.
Her love is my constant support and
her practical commitment to the deprived
and to fashioning a new model of church
is an ever-present challenge
to root my ideas in the realities of
contemporary Ireland.

Contents

Introduction

Thursday, 9 February 1984 was hailed by the Irish media as an historic day. For the first time ever a group of Irish Catholic bishops subjected themselves to public questioning by leading representatives of the Republic's three main political parties and the SDLP from the north. The four bishops, Dr Edward Daly from Derry and Dr Cahal Daly from Down and Connor representing the north, and Dr Joe Cassidy of Clonfert and Dr Dermot O'Mahony, an auxiliary bishop of Dublin, from the south, performed impressively. Many viewers of the public questioning, afterwards broadcast in full on television, could not have failed to be struck by the difference between this reasonable, concerned, friendly and even humorous group of men and the public image of the Irish hierarchy as secretive, reactionary and authoritarian. All in all they came across, in the words of Bishop Cassidy, as 'a rather benign species'.

But if their style was positive and impressive, the three hour public questioning at the New Ireland Forum failed to elicit any clue as to what sort of new Ireland they stood for. Significantly it was the negative statement that the bishops did not seek a confessional Catholic state that dominated the headlines the following morning. Bishop Cahal Daly said they would not stand in the way of any moves to seek a more reconciled, just and peaceful society. They pledged to oppose any constitutional proposals which might infringe or endanger the civil and religious rights and liberties of the northern Protestants. But in response to questions on the thorny issue of whether they would oppose the introduction of divorce legislation in the Republic they resorted to broad, general replies on the evils of divorce. All of this was predictable but it told us more about what they were against rather than what they were for.

Even more important, however, is what the bishops omitted. Nowhere in their written submission to the Forum did they address themselves to the major issue of injustice in Ireland and how they seek to build a more just society. One got the impression from listening to them that the only area of injustice they perceive is the alienation of the Catholic minority from the institutions of the Northern Ireland state. But their perceptive and important contribution on this issue highlighted the fact that when their repeated delegations to British ministers failed to achieve concessions they saw no alternative way of countering what Bishop Edward Daly admitted was the effectiveness of violent means in forcing government reforms.

For a group whom we are constantly told by the media hold immense power, the bishops came across as quite bereft of positive ideas and vision. Indeed the impression created was that the most they have to offer the growth of a new Ireland is the preservation of certain values about family life, even though the tide of public opinion is clearly moving against them in this area. For all the good humour and sweet reasonableness, the clear result of the public questioning was a conviction that the leaders of the Catholic Church will at best be a minimal influence in creating a new society on this island.

Such a conclusion is an accurate reflection of the state of the Irish Catholic Church. Still living off the fact that it maintains the allegiance of the majority of the people, the Church has by and large not yet awakened to the major challenge that faces it if it is to find any significant role for itself in the fast-changing Ireland now taking shape. Already the uniquely high rates of Mass-going are declining at a fast-accelerating rate while most who continue to go to Mass show little strong conviction about their Christian faith. The same week as the bishops met the New Ireland Forum an event occurred which more accurately portrayed the way the Church functions in Irish society. A young teacher from New Ross who had been dismissed from her job at a convent secondary school having had a child by a previously married man with whom she was living for some time lost an appeal against her dismissal. This incident indicated the underlying priorities which again and again recur in Irish church life. Sexual transgressions warrant an unhealthy obsession among many Irish Catholics almost to the point where they are seen as unpardonable and to the exclusion of any moral sensitivity to issues such as the growing levels of exploitation and injustice in our society. The result often is that more importance is attached in practice to maintaining the legal forms of marriage and sexual propriety than to fostering stable and loving relationships. Meanwhile the fast growing young population of contemporary Ireland is influenced less and less by such priorities, regarding them as at best irrelevant and at worst blatant hypocrisy.

Pope John Paul II said in Dublin at the beginning of his Irish visit in September 1979 that: 'We cannot live on the glories of our past Christian history.' There is every indication that Irish Catholicism still largely continues to do so. The very strength of the Church in the past, being a Church of the mass of the people, now seems to be its weakness since it seems afraid to challenge those masses to a deeper Christian commitment for fear of losing their allegiance. The end result is a Church largely unsure of what message it has to preach and still relying far too much on a set of priorities which speak little to the needs of Irish people today. On the one issue on which they have taken a strong stand, opposing the liberalisation of laws on sexual morality, Church leaders have failed to do more than delay such liberalisation and have seen growing sectors of the population oppose their views.

With all the evidence of a major crisis facing the Church, it is remarkable just how little this is being examined in public. The Church is not unique in this regard. In any area of Irish life, from our models of economic development to our town planning, and from our television programmes to our educational methods, we tend to import our ideas uncritically from outside. Easily seduced by what appear attractive and painless solutions to our problems coming from the United States and Western Europe, we find ourselves applying solutions little adapted to our own distinctive problems. Thus we have sought to develop our economy by luring in giant multinational companies, whom we pay a fortune to come here, with little regard to the long-term dependence or the social injustice this is creating. Even after twenty years of relying on this model we are subjecting it to remarkably little critical examination. In the poorest and most underdeveloped of Third

World countries one would find far more critical assessment of the role of multinationals and far more creative ideas about alternative models of economic development than one ever finds here in Ireland. We still find it very difficult to look at ourselves as we really are and to have the confidence to fashion our own responses to our problems and be open to the lessons of elsewhere but certainly not copying uncritically those closest to hand.

The ways in which we look at the Church are also largely imported. Our theology, with very few exceptions, simply copies the dominant theology in Western Europe and North America. It is only very recently that a few theologians have begun to use our Irish experience, north and south, as the basis for their theological reflection. From almost all media coverage of Church affairs in this country one would be led to believe that the main issue concerning the Irish Catholic Church at the moment is the struggle by an increasingly liberal public to limit the Church's influence in public affairs as much as possible. While this might be important to a certain minority of affluent middle-class people, it fails to take into account the fact that most people still maintain an allegiance to the Church, even if this is weakening. Much evidence points to the fact that while a small minority might seek staunchly to re-create a traditional authoritarian Catholicism, an increasingly significant minority seek a Church that can take a more active role in our public life not defending the values and institutions of the past but challenging and confronting the new forms of injustice emerging in the new Ireland in the way that they see being done by the Church elsewhere in the world. But the liberal bias of our media or of our dominant theology fails to attach much significance to such a view of the Church. Because we think Ireland is a society similar to those of Western Europe, except a bit more retarded in its development, we fail to appreciate the distinctiveness of our own situation.

This is particularly true when it comes to looking at the Catholic Church, which has played such a major role in our public life over the past century and a half. During the last century and into the early part of this one, when the Catholic Church throughout the rest of Europe (including Poland) was on the defensive and losing much of its institutional control and public power, the Irish Church was growing in power and influence. Now, however, at a time when Catholicism elsewhere has begun to enter a period of remarkable renewal and popularity, in Ireland we see it entering a major crisis of confidence. In this situation we very urgently need a distinctive analysis of this unique phenomenon of Irish Catholicism, otherwise we will continue to misunderstand it, ascribing to it a power which it no longer has while obsessively seeking to limit that power at every turn.

It is in order to hold Irish Catholicism up to the light that this book was written. It seeks to do four things. Firstly, it situates the Church in the context of a fast-changing society which is challenging it and looks at the ways the Church itself has sought to adapt to this situation. Secondly, it uncovers what is the true state of belief among Irish Catholics and how strong their allegiance is to the Church. Thirdly, it looks back into history to discover why we have the kind of Church we have. Fourthly, it points the way towards the growth of a new model of Church for the future, drawing on the resources of our native Irish spirituality, alert to the new needs being thrown up by our emerging society and outlining ways the Church should develop to respond to these. I make no apology for writing from a committed position though I seek to be fair and balanced in my presentation. While the detached observer may have a valid insight to offer, on a topic like this I believe the committed observer can uncover much more thoroughly the dynamic of growth that might not be apparent to the detached observer. Furthermore underlying my analysis is a particular understanding of what the Church should be, derived from recent theological writing on the topic, from official Church teaching and from the example of the new forms the Church is taking on in parts of the world where it has been transformed in recent decades. Central to this understanding is a view of the Church as a genuine community of ordinary Christians exploring their faith in ways which challenge them to a more socially committed life and a simplicity of lifestyle. Such a view quickly overcomes the dualism between faith and life which so paralyses Christian faith as lived and understood in Ireland. Transformation of the world and the building of a new society of justice for the oppressed now become central goals to the mission of the Church, carried out not by clerics alone but by all Christians. Prayer and celebration of the sacraments become, in this setting, the active discernment of where God is acting in the world, the real sharing of sorrows and joys in the presence of God and the motivation for renewed commitment. Such a vision of the Church, far from being utopian, is proving in many parts of the world to be in practice the new form of Church which is emerging out of the attempt to embody the gospel anew for the conditions of our times. Though we can only discern the merest seeds of such a Church in Ireland yet, I believe Irish Catholicism will not be an exception to this trend throughout the world. To the extent that it begins to express itself in this form of Church it will come alive again; to the extent that it seeks to perpetuate the past, or merely adapt to a liberal society tacitly agreeing to provide religious services for a largely apathetic people it will become weaker and weaker as at present.

The publication of this book comes at a time, I feel, when significant sectors in the Irish Catholic Church are wakening up to the major crisis confronting them and are searching for new and more creative responses to it. This itself is a hopeful sign for the future. This little book will, I hope, prove useful to readers in understanding that crisis and responding to it in ways that will lead to the emergence of a new model of Church adequate to the demands of our times. I believe the contemporary situation of the Church in Ireland can be accurately summed up in two lines from a popular Irish ballad, 'Come By the Hills':

> . . . Where the past has been lost,
> And the future has still to be won.

It is my fervent wish that this book might make its own modest contribution towards the winning of that future.

1. A Changing Ireland

For many of those who went to see the feature film of Edna O'Brien's *The Country Girls,* on general release throughout the country in the closing months of 1983, the experience was one of glimpsing a past of which they had no personal experience. When the book was released amid a storm of controversy in 1960 almost half of the present population of Ireland had not been born. Therefore the underlying picture of a stagnant society, presided over by a repressive and sexually obsessed Church, from which the young had to flee if they were to find any space to explore and satisfy their own needs seemed to most cinemagoers under the age of twenty-five as foreign as if it were portraying a far-away country.

Certainly few, if any, would have had direct personal experience of the harsh and unyieldingly narrow moral code which had so deeply touched the sexual and emotional lives of previous generations of Irish Catholics. More than likely their contact with priests, nuns and brothers would have been less frequent and also more humane. Being an Irish Catholic for this generation involves little of the trauma, struggle and ambivalence which it did, and often still does, for their parents. Their relationship to the Church is more tenuous and more easy to discard if it becomes a hindrance.

One would have to go back well over 100 years to find a twenty year period during which the life experience of Irish people changed as dramatically and fundamentally as it did from the early 1960s to the early 1980s. In 1965 the historian, TV personality and TD, the late David Thornley, could write that the country was 'at the threshold of a delayed peaceful social revolution'. He would probably be more than surprised if he were still with us to see just how little this revolution has changed the basic institutions of our society. Fianna Fáil, Fine Gael and Labour still dominate the south's politics, the Catholic Church remains powerful and dominant and the division between nationalist and unionist, though transmuted somewhat, still defines life in the north.

At the deeper level of values and outlook, however, the change has been possibly even more fundamental and radical than David Thornley could have anticipated. More than anything which has happened internally in the Catholic Church over this period, it is the quiet social revolution taking place in Ireland which has eroded the position the Church held in Irish life and in the consciousness of most Irish Catholics. While many conservative Catholics hold the Second Vatican Council (1962-65) responsible for what they see as the weakening of the faith which it introduced, it is unlikely that the reforms of the council alone could have changed the Irish Catholic Church as substantially as has happened. Certainly if the same reforming spirit had motivated the Vatican in the 1940s or 1950s it would have had a very beneficial impact on the Irish Church. But the fact that the changes coincided with so many other changes in Irish life in the mid 1960s made them far more acceptable to a people long schooled in the belief that the Church was a perfect and unchanging society. Though they accepted such changes as Mass in English and Irish, the more simplified and tasteful celebration of the sacraments, the abolition of such traditional disciplines as abstaining from meat on Fridays and, in general, a more relaxed style to the activities and pronouncements of priests and bishops, the quiet revolution taking place in society around them was preparing a far more profound challenge to the faith of the people.

A STAGNANT SOCIETY

It was not as if Ireland had not experienced many changes in the previous 100 years. Such periods as the struggle for the land in the 1880s, the national struggle in the 1910s and 1920s, and the economic war with Britain in the 1930s as the young state struggled to establish itself had all touched the majority of Irish people. These were undoubtedly major watersheds in the social and political life of the country. But their impact on the lives of the people fades into insignificance when compared with the traumatic and sudden reversal of the patterns of social life brought about by the Famine of 1845-48. From having the highest density of population in Western Europe, Ireland suddenly saw its population begin to decline in a process which was not reversed until the 1960s. The country lost a quarter of its people in just one decade, many of them the young and most creative. Those who stayed at home remained mostly on the land living in enforced celibacy until they could inherit the family farm. Those who married did so at a much older age, while there was a decline in the overall proportion of the population which married. Celibacy, whether enforced or chosen in priesthood and religious life, became widespread and even valued in a way it certainly was not thirty years previously. In these factors lay the roots of a stagnant, predominantly rural and sexually puritanical society. The resolution of the land problem in the 1880s and 1890s, with the majority of peasants being allowed to buy out their landholdings, added a political and social conservatism. Thus the achievement of national independence for two-thirds of the island in 1921 did not lead to a fundamental social revolution nor the demand by more than a small minority for it.

With a conservative social base, therefore, Irish society assimilated political changes which in other countries would have caused major social upheavals. This is nowhere more obvious than in the case of the Catholic Church. We will examine in Chapter Five the way the Church was changed and in many ways tamed into becoming the mirror image of the post-Famine society. A stagnant, sexually repressive and conservative society created a stagnant, sexually repressive and conservative Church to give it some meaning. There is nothing strange about this. Every Christian society in history has moulded its dominant Church to give legitimacy to the dominant interests in that society. In recent centuries this has usually meant that the Church served the interests of the rulers while preaching submission to the majority. Ireland was peculiar in that the Church of the majority was not that of the rulers so the Church remained more a Church of the people touching more intimately their lives. Just how dominant it became for the people can be gauged from the almost complete absence of any manifestations in Ireland of the liberal or socialist movements which challenged the Church in neighbouring European societies from the end of the eighteenth century. This absence also confirms that Irish Catholics were, by and large, socially conservative.

At least up until partition in 1920 the presence of a substantial Protestant minority, many of them in positions of power, as well as the fact that the London government held the purse strings in such crucial areas as education, limited to some extent the freedom of action of this conservative brand of Catholicism to mould state legislation and policy in its image. Partition, and the independence of the southern state, changed all that. In a state so predominantly Catholic as was created, there were no influences strong enough to temper Catholic zeal in such areas as contraception, divorce and censorship. Despite such notable exceptions as W. B. Yeats, even the Protestant minority stayed largely silent.

But even more than the restricting effect on legislation, the young state had imposed on it a stifling Catholic nationalist orthodoxy. Expressed in its more positive forms it could be quite appealing as in De Valera's famous St Patrick's Day broadcast of 1943 in which he enunciated his dream that Ireland would be 'the home of a people who valued material wealth only as the basis of a right living, of a people who were satisfied with frugal comfort and devoted their leisure to the things of the spirit. . . in a word, the home of a people living the life that God desires men should live.' There was nothing wrong with the dream; in fact it was far more inspiring and humane than anything we hear from our political leaders today. Rather the problem was that the reality of people's lives, both spiritual and material, bore no relationship to it. It took the writers of the day, alienated as they were from the reality, to give voice to this dichotomy. Terence Brown, in his book *Ireland: A Social and Cultural History 1922-79* expresses this well: 'Instead of De Valera's Gaelic Eden and the uncomplicated satisfactions of Ireland free, the writers revealed a mediocre, dishevelled, often neurotic and depressed petit-bourgeois society that atrophied for want of a liberating idea.' But those who protested were isolated exceptions; the ethos of the state and the conservative Catholicism which underpinned it maintained the solid allegiance of the vast majority of the people.

EMERGING FROM POST-FAMINE IRELAND

This was only finally to change when the stagnant, post-Famine society which had given rise to it changed. The watershed which marks this change is the 1958 First Programme for Economic Expansion. Though symbolised by such important changes as the retirement of Eamon de Valera from active politics in 1959 and the elevation to senior positions of a new and younger generation of politicians who had not fought in the struggle for independence, notably Jack Lynch, Charles J. Haughey, Paddy Hillery, Brian Lenihan and George Colley, much more important was the economic transformation which the new government initiated under the leadership of Seán Lemass as Taoiseach. Through attracting in industry in the form of foreign multi-national companies, Ireland began to experience its industrial revolution. The annual growth rate between 1959 and 1963, which the First Plan envisaged would be two per cent instead, reached four per cent. For the first time since the Famine, the census of 1966 showed an increase in the population and a slow-down in the rate of emigration. With the influx of industry the numbers employed in agriculture began to decline while the population of the cities and towns showed substantial increases. The new economic opportunities also marked the end of the low marriage rates which had begun at the time of the Famine and the number of marriages rose by over 40% between 1958 and 1970.

These changes, though less dramatic than many others which took place since the Famine, were to prove much more profound. The new prosperity and growth led to a new optimism for the future and inspired a searching and altogether new critique of the familiar institutions and landmarks in Irish life. The opening of a national television station on New Year's Eve 1962 facilitated such a critique but it was the fiftieth anniversary of the 1916 Rising which saw the most sustained onslaught on the old orthodoxy. The state's view of itself as embodying the fulfilment of the Irish people's struggle for freedom was replaced by an increasing embarrassment at the more overt forms of Gaelic and nationalist culture. Under the traumatic impact of the northern crisis, the majority in the south was forced silently to re-evaluate even the previously cherished dream of re-unification. The Irish language too was relegated to the status of a private interest instead of its previous importance as the first national language with the state committed to its revival. While none of these aspirations were in theory dropped, their realisation was relegated to some far distant future. Remarkably this rapid demolition of the previously untouchable sacred cows of Irish life met with little opposition and even Fianna Fáil, the political party which had been most overtly committed to a Gaelic, nationalist Ireland, seemed to make the transition to the new liberal orthodoxy almost without noticing. A new, more liberal, Ireland was being born.

Though on the surface the Catholic Church too seemed to make the transition with its uniquely high rates of Mass-going and its dominant role in Irish life virtually untouched, the new ethos was creating a more profound challenge to Christian belief than was recognised. On one level this came with the more open and questioning atmosphere in Ireland. People were being influenced by new ideas, often very critical of the simple religious faith held by most Irish Catholics. The Saturday night *Late Late Show* on television became, in the late 1960s and early 1970s, something akin to an alternative teaching authority to that of the Church, systematically stimulating discussion and dissent on issues of moral and religious belief which most Irish Catholics had previously never questioned. Rarely did this involve an overt attack on Catholic faith. Rather the presenter, Gay Byrne, actually got a number of more liberal priests to provoke the discussion. In a certain sense, this showed the continuing hold of Irish Catholicism in that its authority had to be invoked even to allow the questioning of issues. But, once begun, the process of questioning was soon applied to Catholicism itself and to its moral beliefs, particularly by the young, and before long it became clear that large sectors of the population were paying little attention to the Church's view, even on issues such as contraception and divorce where the conservative Catholic view was staunchly defended by Church leaders. Despite the continuing domination of secondary schooling by the Church, young people were being more influenced by a liberal outlook on life.

This liberalisation of opinion and the weakening of Church authority which followed from it were the inevitable result of the social changes already taking place. In many ways they could be seen as the Irish version of a process which had taken place in Britain, France, Italy and West Germany in the years following the Second World War. It is worth remembering, however, that in other countries, such as the United States, where the Church had been strongly influenced by Irish Catholicism with its dependence on the authority of the priest and its greater stress on a devotional life than on a questioning faith, Catholics had also to wait for the changes of the Vatican Council in the late 1960s before being opened up to a process of probing their faith.

Ireland was unique, however, in that this liberalisation coincided with another result of the changing nature of Irish society, the growth of a consumer society. Not only did most Irish people have more money in the 1960s than they had ever had before but a sophisticated advertising industry developed rapidly in order to convince them to spend it on buying more and more products, from motor cars to foreign holidays, from the latest fashions in clothes to so-called labour saving gadgets. Underlying this advertising was a new view of the world, totally at variance with the Christian faith held by the majority. This view stressed that happiness lay in having more and more and in satisfying one's own needs, even at the expense of others. In its more elaborate forms it created a whole industry to manipulate the young through glossy magazines, fashion boutiques, music and entertainment. Women too were singled out as a group for whom special needs could be created on which they would then have to spend their money.

Again this posed no overt attack on the Christian faith of the majority. In fact its success lay in the subtle way it influenced the

whole population most of whom would have felt no tension
between living or aspiring to a lifestyle of affluence and comfort
and the basic call of the gospel to a lifestyle of simplicity and
solidarity. This is graphically illustrated in the way that the Christian feast of Christmas, the celebration of the birth of our God
in poverty, has been transmuted into a feast of lavish consump-
tion. Through the constant propaganda of advertising, consump-
tion – the buying of goods and products beyond anything one
might reasonably need – became a new god for many Irish people.
This now was their most important value in life with happiness
and fulfilment dependent on it.

The constant pressure to consume had led different social
groups to react in different ways. For the new urban poor, particularly those young people condemned to the aimlessness and depri-
vation of unemployment, theft and vandalism have become their
understandable reaction. For the new rich, at the other end of
the scale, quick and massive profits are possible through specula-
tion in land and buildings or through playing the stock exchange.
Far too often it is the former who bear the brunt of moral condemnation while the far greater immorality of the latter has taken on
almost an aura of respectability.

NEW PRESSURES

Though there have been many beneficial results from the new
prosperity experienced by most Irish people over the past two
decades and few would wish for a return to the austerity and
stagnation preceding it, it has also engendered its own pressures
and problems. This has led to the widespread phenomenon of
urban loneliness and alienation. Without the community sup-
ports which existed in the more rural and stable society of yester-
day, many women with young families left in the home all day,
or single people living alone, resort to drugs. When these are the
socially accepted variety like alcohol or drugs prescribed by
doctors, the underlying problems they suggest tend to be overlooked. It is only the huge problem of dependence on illegal and
highly destructive drugs like heroin which alerts us to the fact

that many people find living in our society very difficult to cope with.

Unlike their predecessors, it is these individual problems with meaning and identity which dominate the work of contemporary Irish artists and writers. With few exceptions 'they resolutely continued to explore the private worlds of their own obsessions,' said Terence Brown in reference to Irish writers over the past twenty years. Ultimately it is this retreat into the private and the abdication of responsibility for the kind of searing and hard-hitting social critique in which previous generations of Irish writers and artists excelled which is a major characteristic of Irish society today. Private dreams predominate over social vision in the new Ireland.

Irish Catholicism therefore finds itself, for the first time in its long existence, living in an environment which is subtly undermining it. It has been forced to live in a hostile environment before and, if anything, those long years of persecution strengthened it. The process now is altogether more ambiguous because many of the changes of the past twenty years have undoubtedly made Ireland a more humane and positive place to live in. The Catholic Church has, in many cases, welcomed and even helped to achieve some of these changes. But they have also brought an environment which makes new demands on the faith of the people and challenges it in ways it has little experience of. The way it responded was to show whether it grasped this as an opportunity for conversion or a threat to be resisted.

READING

Terence Brown, *Ireland; A Social and Cultural History, 1922-79.* Fontana, Glasgow, 1981.

Desmond Fennell, *The State of the Nation.* Ward River Press, Dublin, 1983.

F. S. L. Lyons, *Ireland Since the Famine.* Fontana, Glasgow, 1973.

Louis McRedmond, 'The Church in Ireland', in *The Church Now,* eds. John Cumming and Paul Burns, Gill and Macmillan, Dublin, 1980.

John A. Murphy, *Ireland in the Twentieth Century.* Gill and Macmillan, Dublin, 1975.

2. Adapting to Change

In his address to the students of Maynooth during his visit to Ireland in late 1979 Pope John Paul II urged: 'You must work for the Lord with a sense of urgency. You must work with the conviction that this generation, this decade of the 1980s which we are about to enter, could be crucial and decisive for the future of the faith in Ireland.' The Pope emphasised again and again in every major address he gave the idea that 'Ireland is at a point of decision in her history'. Amid the euphoria of the moment it appeared to be lost on the majority of his listeners.

Though many senior Irish bishops made important contributions to the content of these addresses, the note of urgency about the present situation evident in them contrasted strongly with the caution which has so dominated the Irish bishops' conference in recent years. Far from showing any urgency about change in the Church, most Irish bishops gave the impression of accepting change reluctantly and only because it was demanded by Rome in the aftermath of the Second Vatican Council. Such changes were loyally implemented though by and large with little enthusiasm on the part of most clergy. But the spirit underlying them, summed up in the new image of the Church as the 'People of God', was rarely understood. While elsewhere in the Catholic world this new image was inspiring lay people to see themselves as equal members of the Church alongside the clergy, and was leading to an altogether more positive appreciation of the role of the Church in making the world a better place to live in, the Irish Church maintained an emphasis on fulfilling the law, obeying authority and saving one's soul. Because more used to dominating a submissive laity than in co-operating with them in the task of fashioning a more Christian Church, most Irish priests and bishops remained as blind to the possibilities offered by the reforms of the Council as they were to the new challenges being posed to the faith of the majority. The reforms of the Second

Vatican Council were introduced therefore into a Church which did not really feel the need for them.

UPDATING THE INSTITUTION

Of all the changes introduced in the late 1960s and early 1970s, the ones which affected most churchgoers were the changes in the liturgy. The transition from the Latin Mass, which the congregation 'heard' largely in uncomprehending silence, to the Mass in English and Irish, in which the congregation was expected to take an active part, was probably effected with more success in Ireland than in almost any other country. While many may have regretted the passing of what they loved so much, there was no organised backlash in the form of a Latin Mass Society as happened in Britain, for example. The quality of obedience remained stronger among the Irish than any defence of what was seen by some as an essential aspect of Catholicism. But neither were the possibilities offered by the new liturgy exploited in any real way in most Irish parishes and the Mass in English or Irish continued to be celebrated in a dull and uninspiring way with little active participation by the people.

It was in other areas that the reforms inspired by the Vatican Council bore most fruit in the Irish Church. Undoubtedly the most outstanding success has been *Trocaire,* the largest of the many bishops' commissions set up to co-ordinate and oversee different aspects of the ministry of the Irish Church. *Trocaire* was founded in 1973 as the Irish Catholic agency for world development and since then it has carved out for itself a leading place among similar agencies throughout the world. Discriminating in the groups to which it gives aid in the Third World, it has won praise from leading bishops abroad for supporting those groups seeking to help themselves and addressing the root causes of their underdevelopment. Neither has *Trocaire* neglected the more sensitive area of educating the public at home to the causes of world injustice and criticising successive governments for their niggardly aid contributions to the Third World, activities which have involved it in controversy with both politicians and other aid agencies. It has played a major role in developing a public awareness of the political and economic injustices which cause and perpetuate underdevelopment particularly in Central America, southern Africa and the Philippines. It is a remarkable achievement for a Church which has been little noted for having a developed social conscience.

But the equivalent groups set up to tackle injustice at home cannot be said to have shown the same vigour. The Irish Commission for Justice and Peace, a much smaller group than *Trocaire*, has concentrated its attention largely on introducing a dimension of education for justice and peace in the school curricula and on producing publications for the use of adult groups. In these publications it has shown the links between disarmament and world development and has popularised the conclusions of the Brandt Report on reforming the unjust relationship between the rich and poor countries of the world. It also sponsored a critical study of Ireland's development aid. The Council of Social Welfare has more substantial achievements to its credit in developing a public awareness about the extent of poverty in Ireland particularly through its Kilkenny conferences on poverty in 1971 and 1981. In the Council's various statements on social issues, it has embodied concrete recommendations for the development of a comprehensive social policy by the government, in co-operation with research institutes, so as to plan for the elimination of the gross inequalities in Irish society. However, the perspective of helping poor people to help themselves by addressing the root causes of their underdevelopment, which underlies the work of *Trocaire,* is largely missing when the Church begins to look at injustice in Ireland. Rather it looks to the government and the well-off to help the poor.

The teaching of religion, or catechetics as it is called, has been revolutionised since the Vatican Council with the founding of two third-level colleges, Mater Dei Institute in Dublin and Mount Oliver in Dundalk, to train teachers and develop new methods for religious education. These have been the first third-level colleges where Catholic lay people could study theology since the only other courses offered were in seminaries training men for the priesthood. The 'Catholic' colleges of the National University do not offer theology as a subject and it is paradoxical that it was Trinity College, which Catholics were forbidden from attending up to 1970, which has become the first university in the south to offer theology as a subject to lay people. The emergence of a group of lay people more literate in their faith than was possible except in isolated cases up until recently is to be welcomed both because of the badly needed improvements it has led to in the field of religious education but also because it should spearhead a more critical involvement of lay people in the life of the Church.

Other Church institutions which have emerged from this ferment of reform include the Catholic Communications Institute which trains clergy and lay people in the use of radio and television. Associated with this is the well-known *Radharc* team which has travelled the world making highly successful television films about aspects of the life of the Church. In the ecumenical field, apart from regular contacts and meetings between the leadership of the main churches which have produced such notable documents as the inter-church study of violence in Ireland, the annual week of prayer for Christian unity every January has won the active backing of Catholic Church leaders. Though not set up by the Irish bishops, a unique ecumenical institution, the Irish School of Ecumenics, founded in 1970, draws students from all over the world for its courses on the different Christian traditions as well as on non-Christian religions.

Apart from the various institutions established, the past two decades have also seen a notable change in the issues to which the Irish bishops address themselves as well as in the style they adopt. While Bishop Eamonn Casey of Galway is not typical, his outspoken stand on such issues as American intervention in Central America or the nuclear arms race exemplify a radical new style in contrast to the reserve and aloofness which has characterised most Irish Catholic bishops. Such major documents of the bishops' conference as the pastoral letters *Human Life is Sacred* (1975) and *The Work of Justice* (1977) or the two statements issued during 1983, one on nuclear weapons and the other

on the economic recession, indicate not just a wider set of interests
than before but also a more positive tone. This emphasises that
Catholics have a duty to work for a better society, to analyse and
confront injustice in its many forms and to translate their practice
of religion into more effective concern for the deprived. As J. H.
Whyte says in his definitive study *Church and State in Modern
Ireland 1923-79*: 'The hierarchy could now be classified as a
left-of-centre critic of Irish society.'

RESISTING CHANGE

However, that is far from how they are still perceived in the
public consciousness. Ask any average young Irish person as to
what moral issue most worries the Catholic bishops and they
will not reply social injustice or nuclear war but rather sexual
immorality. For no matter how many statements might have been
issued on other matters it is on issues concerning the liberalisation
of laws related to sexual morality and marriage that Irish Catholic
bishops as a group have been seen to take up a crusading attitude
over the past decade.

The 1970s were dominated in this regard by the debate on the
legalisation of the sale of contraceptives. But though the bishops
consistently and repeatedly opposed it, the tide of legislative opinion swung steadily against them as the decade progressed. The
first contraception bill, introduced in the Seanad by three inde-
pendent members in 1971 did not even receive a first reading.
By 1973 the opinion of the upper house had changed enough to
grant a first reading to a similar bill. But it was the Supreme
Court ruling in the Magee case in the same year, declaring the
ban on the importation of contraceptives unconstitutional, which
forced a reluctant legislature to grasp the nettle. By the time a
new law was finally passed in 1979, restricting the sale of contraceptives to married couples, it was clear that public opinion
was largely in favour of the measure.

The bishops did not relent in their opposition and statements
of the bishops' conferences in 1973, 1976, 1978 and 1980 all
argued strongly against not just the idea of liberalising the law

but even the restrictive Haughey bill which was finally passed. Indeed the final statement of the four, issued after the bill had become law, began an offensive to prevent further liberalisation and supported the right of doctors and pharmacists to refuse to prescribe or sell contraceptives under the bill. Aware that public opinion was moving against them, however, the bishops introduced what proved to be a very important clause in the 1973 statement saying that the Church had never expected state law to mirror Catholic teaching. 'Those who insist on seeing the issue purely in terms of the state enforcing, or not enforcing, Catholic moral teaching are missing the point,' the bishops said. The real point, they argued, was the impact on society which a change in the law would be likely to have. However, the bishops' arguments on these grounds against the law tended to be largely overlooked in favour of what was seen at the time as a tacit episcopal nod in the direction of the politicians to get on with the matter if they had to. The bishops' assertion that 'no one had ever suggested, least of all the Church herself' that state law should prohibit what the Catholic Church forbids met with not a little surprise since over the previous fifty years both bishops and legislators had frequently acted on the assumption that the laws of a 'Catholic' state should mirror Catholic teaching.

The bishops' clarification on this issue, therefore, can only be seen as a retreat in the face of the steady liberalisation of public opinion. A similar clarification at the time of the 1951 Mother and Child controversy might have saved the coalition government of the day from collapse. But with public opinion as deferential to the bishops as were the politicians at the time most of the people expected their legislators to follow episcopal advice. By the 1970s this was no longer true and the contraception controversy of that decade marks the beginning of the Catholic bishops seeing themselves as one pressure group among many others in the state, but with an influence over public opinion which far outweighs that of any other pressure group when it comes to matters of sexual morality.

The referendum on amending the constitution in relation to the rights of the unborn in 1983 indicated for the first time, however, the emergence of new liberal pressure groups challenging the Church for dominance even on these issues. While the statement of the bishops' conference on the referendum recognised the rights of Catholics to vote against the proposal, numerous individual bishops as well as local priests throughout the country urged Catholics in the strongest terms to vote in favour. Thus the fact that only half the electorate voted at all, and only one third of the total electorate voted in favour, indicates a growing inability on the part of the Church to influence public opinion even on what it regards as fundamental issues. Perhaps the most worrying result of the referendum, from the bishops' point of view, was the opinion poll taken just a few days before the vote which correctly predicted the result but which also showed a 60% majority in favour of legalising divorce. The steady liberalisation of public opinion, as well as the open disagreement between senior politicians and the bishops which emerged during the referendum campaign, makes it likely that as the politicians begin to tackle the issue of divorce during the 1980s they will pay far less heed to the opposition of the bishops than was the case in the 1970s.

The other issue on which the Catholic Church was seen to take a strong stand in the 1970s was over control of schooling. The traditional dominance of the Church in this area was challenged by the introduction of community schools in the early 1970s when the vocational sector, previously under lay control, and the teachers' unions challenged the right of Church officials to nominate a majority of the board of management as had been originally agreed between the Department of Education and the Church. Though it fought hard for as much control as possible, the Church had finally to compromise.

LACK OF PASTORAL STRATEGY

Despite the many new institutions set up or the new issues on which statements were made, therefore, the 1970s showed that most Irish Church leaders were not aware that a deeper challenge faced them. At heart their priorities remained very traditional and though welcoming change in theory when that change affected what they saw as their vital interests they proved doggedly resistant to it. The results were little short of disastrous. In defending a Catholic school system they alienated the lay teaching profession on whom they will have to depend to run that system as the number of priests and religious continues to decline. In their resistance to liberalising the laws on sexual matters they seemed blind to the increasing public support for such liberalisation and thus the inevitability of it happening. Through their stand on these issues they cast themselves in the role of the stubborn defenders of a traditional society thus losing much public goodwill. Paradoxically the end result appears to be that any episcopal statement, even those on issues like social justice and nuclear disarmament which should receive a wide welcome, are usually met with cynicism and dismissal.

That the challenge of a changing society demanded not just new and updated institutions but a whole new role in society, a new pastoral strategy, never seemed to strike the bishops. Only once did they address themselves to this issue, at a meeting at Mulrany in Co. Mayo in 1974. But the resulting document, called *Pastoral Guidelines,* betrays a very traditional understanding of the Church's pastoral role. It involves no evaluation of the failure of the traditional methods used by the Church to preach its message and thus rests content with minor recommendations for improving the pastoral care of priests and families. Though the guidelines state that 'the main thrust of the Irish Church over the next five years should be the implementation of the principle of involvement of the laity' the bishops do not lay out any means through which this is to be implemented. Not surprisingly it has largely remained a dead letter.

Instead the underlying pastoral strategy of the Irish Church has continued to rely on religious education in schools to give some Christian formation to young Catholics, to maintain the people's faith through going to Mass every Sunday and to uphold moral standards on sexual matters and a strong family life through opposing the liberalisation of laws on contraception, divorce and abortion. Such a strategy treats the lay people as the objects of the Church's action rather than, as the Second Vatican Council does, seeing them as the body of the Church helped by the clergy to develop their faith and their Christian action in society. This was most clearly expressed in Pope John Paul II's visit to Ireland. While the visit was a magnificent success on one level with the Pope endearing himself to many Irish people, his talks were dominated by this basic pastoral strategy. Where he added significant emphases of his own, such as his repeated stress on the duty of Catholics to identify and eliminate social injustice or his urge to promote the role of the laity in the life of the Church, they tended to be overlooked if not in theory at least in practice. The visit appeared as an attempt by Church leaders to overawe the wavering back into the practice of their faith. It was a short-sighted approach which could not substitute for a more humble attempt to discern the deeper needs of the new generation emerging in Ireland and make a more creative response to these.

While many priests and bishops do their best to help develop an adult faith among the people, they do so through outmoded parish structures which often hinder rather than help this process. Most make little attempt to develop new forms of ministry. Indeed, as the National Conference of Priests of Ireland said at their 1981 annual meeting: 'Many priests do not have the vision of the Church central to Vatican II. There is little involvement of the laity, lack of team work in ministry, and a complacent acceptance of the status quo.' In adapting the Church to a new society the Irish bishops have not yet addressed themselves to these problems in any coherent way and are far from even recognising the extent of the problem. They have been more concerned with maintaining the institutions functioning rather than with fostering new forms of mission through which this generation of Irish people could be excited by a vision of what it is to be a Christian. While they devoted their attention to updating institutions and expanding the parish network in new urban areas little was being done to prevent the slow but steady erosion of the faith of the average young Irish Catholic. Because they were kept so busy with administering institutions most Irish Church leaders failed to notice the emerging crisis.

READING

J. H. Whyte, *Church and State in Modern Ireland 1923-1979*. 2nd edition, Gill and Macmillan, Dublin, 1980.

3. Faith in Crisis

In a major article published in 1974, a Jesuit priest lecturing in University College Dublin, Fr Michael Paul Gallagher, drew public attention for the first time to what he called 'the possible slow death of Irish Catholicism'. The article, called 'Atheism Irish Style' (*The Furrow,* April 1974), urged some recognition for the fact 'that significant numbers of young people are losing any living contact with both Christ and the Church'.

However, Fr Gallagher's attempt to awaken Church leaders to the growing crisis of faith in their midst was not helped by the publication, in the same year, of the initial results of the first ever comprehensive survey of religious attitudes and beliefs in Ireland. The survey, carried out in 1973-74 by the Council for Research and Development, a commission which had been set up by the bishops themselves, confirmed that Ireland's uniquely high rates of church-going and belief in God remained as high as ever. The survey found that 91% of the Irish Catholics attended Mass every week, 95% believed in God and 97% prayed at some time every day. Such statistics were used a lot by Church leaders in the following years to bolster their belief that all was basically well in the Irish Church.

MAJOR CRISIS

But a closer look at the statistics bore out Fr Gallagher's contention that a major crisis lay just beneath the surface. This was emphasised in the conclusions of a working party, set up by the bishops and including such prominent figures as Mr Frank Cluskey TD, then leader of the Labour party, Dr Laurence Forrestal, then a parish priest in Dublin and now bishop of Ossory and Mr Padraic White of the Industrial Development Authority. This working party, which met in 1977-78, examined some of the pastoral implications of the survey. Their report highlighted that among young people in their early twenties only 78% go to Mass weekly while they estimated that for young men living in large towns and cities the number of those who miss weekly Mass could be as high as 50%. Similarly they stressed that only 19% of young people (between the ages of 18 to 30) received communion weekly while 33% of young men receive it less than once a year. Six out of every ten young people agreed that one can be a good Catholic without going to Mass on Sundays. Thus, the working party said: 'It is almost like two different worlds existing side by side, each unaware of the other's existence. It is this other story which would justify concern for the future of Irish Catholicism.' The report identifies three categories of people among whom Mass attendance and religious belief is declining – the young, people living in large towns or cities and skilled or semi-skilled workers. These are the groups which are growing in numbers and importance in Irish society, the report points out, while the groups among whom Church affiliation is strongest – older, rural and less well educated people – are on the decline.

Even among those who maintain strong religious beliefs and practice the motivation is largely legalistic. Of respondents in the survey who thought missing Sunday Mass always wrong, 46.6% gave their reason as the law of God or similar, 22.7% as duty and 23.6% gave no reason. On the other hand only 26% admitted to having had a religious experience while only 16% said they found religion helpful in time of stress. The survey found that 32% had difficulty with some aspect of the Church's teaching. This figure rose to 47.5% for the young. Similarly, though the survey found 25% of Irish Catholics had a low level of religious outlook, the figure rose to 61% for young men. The working party concluded that: 'This appears to indicate that, for many, the practice of religion is more a matter of law/routine/social pressure, rather than a result of intellectual and personal conviction.'

Legalism was also identified as the major motivation in the area of morality: 'A majority of Irish Catholics see morality as keeping rules/laws rather than as a commitment to values.' With the breakdown of legalism as a restraining factor in sexual behaviour, the survey found that three out of every four young people living in cities regard extra-marital sex as not always wrong. On the issue of contraception, which had been repeatedly condemned by the Church in the years immediately preceding the survey due to the papal encyclical *Humanae Vitae* of 1968 in which Pope Paul VI had re-iterated the Church's opposition to artificial contraception, the survey found that 49% of young men and 45% of young women disagreed with the Church's teaching. The working party concluded: 'There is a great pastoral danger that the legalistic pattern will be substituted by a void of amoral attitudes unless the Church becomes aware of the nature of the problem she is facing.'

Thus the picture emerged of a growing number of people who continue to practice their religion but pay little heed to its moral teachings. This was pointed out by Fr Liam Ryan, professor of sociology at Maynooth, in an article ('Faith Under Survey', *The Furrow*, January 1983) in which he examined the results of all the different surveys done in Ireland over the past decade into belief and practice among Catholics. These showed that one-third of Catholics said that religious principles seldom if ever guide their behaviour, a figure which increases to 55% for the city-born and 61% for the young. Only 28% would put the demands of religion first if they clashed with the interests of family, work or even recreation. This indicates the growing weakness of the Church, summed up in the working party report: 'The clear trend among the younger age groups is towards a marginalisation of religion into a ritualised practice. Religion appears as a fringe activity of one's private life.'

The comforting picture of high Mass-going which emerged in the 1973-74 survey appears on closer inspection, therefore, as largely illusory, lulling Church leaders into a false sense of complacency and hiding the growing crisis beneath the surface. This crisis was recognised and graphically expressed in a report written by a missionary priest who returned to Ireland having worked for ten years in the Philippines. Upon completing a five year assignment here before going abroad again, he wrote: 'There is a spiritual malnutrition behind the impressive Church practice in Ireland. In Ireland, the immediate danger to faith is not unbelief but shallow faith. . . The danger is that religion will be reduced to a minor leisure time activity, a convention retained but only on the margins of life, something devoid of challenge or depth. Because of the drastically changed outer context in Irish society, Sunday practice need no longer lead to a strong faith; a full church could be the opium of the clergy; it could blind one not only to the growing absenteeism, but to the hidden spiritual malnutrition of those present.'

In the decade since the first survey there have been many others looking at specific groups such as university students, secondary school students or Dublin adults. All have confirmed the picture presented above. In the absence of another national survey of the same type as the first (though a similar one is being planned for 1984-85) the survey done in Ireland for the European Values Study Group in late 1980 presents a more up-to-date picture of Church practice. This showed that the overall practice rate had fallen to 82% while among young people it was down to 72%. Interestingly this contrasts with the projection made by the 1977-78 working party on the basis of trends in the 1973-74 survey that by 1986 Sunday Mass-going would have dropped to 85% overall and to 79% among the young. Therefore, it appears that the drop in Mass-going is accelerating, a view which is borne out by reports from some priests in working class Dublin parishes who estimate that only 10% of their parishioners go to Mass every Sunday. In a survey done by Sr. Bernadette MacMahon among teenagers in a number of Dublin schools, she found that while 78% went to Sunday Mass until the age of 15, by the age of 17 the rate among the same teenagers had dropped to 64%.

POWER SHARING

These clear trends, therefore, led the working party to recommend 'immediate and concerted pastoral planning' by Irish Church leaders. While it might be claimed that some attempt has been made to develop a deeper moral maturity among school pupils through a new style religious education, it is much more difficult to see any significant or rapid moves, as called for in the report, towards the genuine involvement of the laity not just in doing things for the priest but in actually helping to run the parish community. Recent research shows just how shortsighted this is, even from the standpoint of the declining numbers of Church personnel to serve a growing population. The numbers of priests, sisters and brothers have shown a steady decline since 1970. In that year the total number was 33,092 while in 1983 it was down to 28,607. In every year since 1974, when these statistics first began to be compiled at a national level, the numbers of deaths or departures from the ranks have far exceeded the number of entrants. Another important factor is the age structure of Church personnel. Whereas in 1970 40% were under the age of 40 and 41% were over the age of 50, by 1981 only 25% were under 40 and 55% over 50. Smaller numbers of young priests, sisters and brothers have to support ever larger numbers of older ones. This is going to be a major drain on the financial resources and freedom of action of many religious orders in years to come.

But the working party report identifies much more important reasons for the active involvement of the laity in the life of the Church. It highlights the survey's findings that a large percentage of Catholics see their Church leaders as being out of touch with the real needs of the people and, furthermore, say that 'it may well be that it is the clergy, rather than the laity, who are more opposed to change within the structures of the Church.' It is an obvious conclusion, therefore, that the Church has little hope of addressing itself to the needs of the new generation of Irish people until it facilitates the laity to become actively involved at all levels of Church life. In stressing the fact that the laity should no longer be treated as second class citizens in a Church dominated by the clergy but should instead be equal partners in fashioning new Church structures to meet the challenges of our day, the working party was doing no more than applying the vision of the Second Vatican Council to the Irish situation. If it has succeeded in applying other aspects of the Council's vision to Ireland, however, in this central aspect the Church has completely failed.

For this the clergy are not entirely to blame. While they have, by and large, resisted sharing their almost absolute power in

Church life with the laity there have been few examples of lay movements demanding greater involvement. Most Irish Catholics seem to resist a more active involvement in Church life and almost resent it on the rare occasion it is asked of them. In comparing surveys of Catholics in England and Wales with those in Ireland (*Doctrine and Life,* December 1981), Máire Nic Ghiolla Phádraig points to the fact that while Mass-going levels are much higher in Ireland, active involvement in the Church as gauged by the membership of parish organisations is much higher in England and Wales than in Ireland. Overall 13% of English and Welsh Catholics, and almost 19% of those who have some connection to a parish, are members of a parish organisation while only 5.6% of Irish Catholics are as involved in the life of their Church. The fact that English and Welsh Catholics, being a minority, possibly have more sociological reasons for identifying with their parish in no way lessens its significance. This finding is confirmed by the experience of members of the bishops' Commission for the Laity here who have had little success in establishing enduring lay groups in the dioceses they represent.

Most lay Catholic organisations in Ireland, with a few notable exceptions, date from before the Second Vatican Council and continue to embody a very traditional vision of the role of the laity in the Church. This is most evident in the case of the most important lay movement to have emerged from the Irish Church, the Legion of Mary. When it was founded in 1921, the Legion spearheaded a more active involvement of lay people in the pastoral work of the Church and had a major impact on the emerging Churches in many Third World countries. Since the 1960s it has been on the decline, however, due to its stubborn refusal to adapt its structures to a new situation. A long-established Catholic movement which has adapted well in recent years is the St Vincent de Paul Society which has seen a steady growth in its membership, especially among the young. But it remains an exception. Such groups as the different Third Orders, the Knights of Columbanus, the Guild of Catholic Nurses and numerous sodalities and altar societies throughout the country continue to represent by far the largest numbers of Catholics active in lay organisations but have

little to contribute to young people anxious to fashion a new
Church responsive to their needs. Even more right-wing is the
secretive Opus Dei which, though it has only about 750 members
in Ireland, has a policy of recruiting wealthy and influential
people which gives it an influence in Irish life beyond its numerical
strength.

The last decade has seen a major growth in groups which help
deepen the spiritual life of their members. Foremost among these
is the Charismatic Renewal which began in Ireland in 1972 and
reached the peak of its growth in 1981 with almost 450 prayer
groups throughout the country. The membership of these groups
varied from 25 to 200. Fr Martin Tierney, who worked full-time
for three and a half years with the movement, credits it with
having helped thousands of lay people to recognise for the first
time that they had spiritual gifts to lead others to prayer and a
deeper experience of God. Though predominantly lay, numerous
priests and sisters have also experienced a new depth to prayer
through the Renewal. Similarly other groups such as Marriage
Encounter, the Christian Family Movement, Focalare, the Christian Life Communities and Teams of Our Lady have contributed
to deepening the spirituality of individuals and families. The
opening of numerous new retreat houses throughout the country
has helped provide much needed facilities that further the same
process.

However, it now appears that this process of deepening individual spirituality will either develop a more socially conscious
commitment or begin to decline. Fr Michael Paul Gallagher sees
it as a necessary stage through which people can move from a
very legalistic Christianity to a more socially committed one. Its
dangers are highlighted by Fr Tierney who criticises the Charismatic Renewal for fostering 'a very cosy Christianity' and he
worries about the resistance of many in the movement to examin-
ing the social implications of the gospel. This emerged in the
numerous criticisms of members to articles in the movement's
magazine, *New Creation,* which examined aspects of injustice at
home and abroad.

MISSING LINKS

While both the traditional Catholic groups and the new move-ments of spiritual growth may have helped thousands upon thousands of people to live more Christian lives they have made little contribution to fashioning new Church structures more adapted to the needs of a new society. They proved completely incapable of taking up documents like the Irish bishops' pastoral letter on justice in 1977 or recent papal documents on the same topic, educating their own members in them or translating them into effective action for social change. Parish life has remained dominated by a clergy often little inclined to treat most lay people as equal partners with themselves. The Irish Church has been characterised by the complete absence of the new lay communities – often called basic Christian communities – which have become the principal means through which lay Catholics throughout Latin America, Western Europe, North America and parts of Africa and Asia have begun to discover the more liberating dimen-sions of their faith and commit themselves to the struggles for a more just society. Furthermore, despite the presence of numerous enthusiastic and well-educated lay Catholics who would welcome the opportunity to work full-time in the pastoral ministry of the Church, the great majority of lay people employed by the Church in Ireland spend their time behind desks. There must be no other majority Church in any country in the world which does not employ lay people to work in pastoral teams with priests and sisters and to contribute their creativity in fashioning a whole variety of new Church structures to preach and embody the gospel effectively for the men and women of our time.

Another pertinent sign of the subordinate place of the laity in the Irish Church is the absence of any magazine or newspaper through which they could be made aware of the variety of new structures and movements emerging in the Church worldwide, introduced to the fement of ideas concerning the Church and its role in society, given a voice to articulate their own ideas and find out about what new initiatives are emerging within the Irish Church. Existing magazines, such as *Doctrine and Life* and *The*

Furrow have a largely clerical readership while the weekly *Irish Catholic* caters for far too conservative a readership to be able to offer any new vision.

Just a year after the Pope's visit a major Christian youth congress was organised at Maynooth. Bishop Casey called it 'the most significant event to emerge from the Pope's visit' and one of its organisers, Mr John Fennessy, told delegates in his opening address that 'young people must take over the Church'. With some 2,000 young people, delegates sent from parishes all over the country, it was the first ever representative gathering of Irish Catholics. The clergy, including some bishops, came to listen and learn as Bishop Brendan Comiskey put it at the opening Mass.

The congress did indeed mirror the state of the Irish Church. In contrast to the major National Pastoral Congress held in Liverpool the previous May when delegates had been elected by parish groups after numerous discussions about the major problems facing the Church and society, delegates to Maynooth were chosen by their parish priests and had no discussions with local young people to see what issues they wanted raised. The issues which dominated were incredibly narrow and churchy – more involvement in the parish Mass, the need for priests to be more active and in touch with youth, a return to family prayer and better religious education in schools. Even the mild criticisms of clergy voiced by some delegates were resisted by the organising committee. The narrow and defensive vision behind the congress and its basically authoritarian response was shown when the secretary of the Irish Student Christian Movement, Mr Martin Rowan, was threatened with the police for selling his movement's theological publications. The few delegates aware of the strong alienation from the Church felt by many of their peers were marginalised and went unheard. Perhaps the saddest picture to emerge from the congress was one of a Church which had succeeded in moulding young Catholics in the image and likeness of an authoritarian and unaware clergy.

The early 1980s therefore seemed to confirm the fears expressed by the working party of 1977-78: 'The great pastoral danger. . . is that Irish Catholicism is increasingly absent from the major tasks of social, political and human progress which face us. These tasks could be seen as "not really part of the Christian task": the end result would be the retreat of Irish Catholicism into a ghetto of private, and increasingly irrelevant, practices of religion.' Or, put more simply, the Irish church in the early 1980s seems to fulfil the grim warning given by an Irish Columban priest on trial in the Philippines, Fr Niall O'Brien, in an article he wrote in *The Furrow* (February 1984): 'Much prayer coupled with little justice guarantees atheism in the next generation.' He could have been describing the Irish church.

READING

Michael Paul Gallagher, SJ, *Help my Unbelief.* Veritas, Dublin, 1983.

Peadar Kirby, 'The Irish Church: The Shifting Sands' in *Doctrine and Life,* October 1977.

4. Northern Ireland: The Final Failure?

Whatever political views Christians may have about the complex problems which rend society apart in Northern Ireland, few can doubt that it is the single greatest challenge which the Churches face in Ireland today. Bishop Cahal Daly has identified violence in the north as 'one of the gravest dangers facing the Church in Ireland at this time. It threatens our religious and spiritual inheritance, our moral values, our family life, the formation of our youth.' A leading Catholic theologian, Fr Enda McDonagh of Maynooth, put the challenge even more starkly when he wrote: 'The very survival of Christianity as a saving force in Irish society may be at stake'. He went on to ask: 'Is Northern Ireland, with its continuing violence and deep-seated religious division, a symbol of the final failure of our conventional Church allegiances and their halting Christianity?'

The question is a sobering one indicating that this particular challenge, because it is bound up so intimately with certain Christian symbols and theologies, may be the definitive test as to whether the Church and even Christian faith itself is any longer an effective force for reconciliation and liberation in our society. The Northern Ireland situation is also challenging for another reason. For in facing other issues, whether Church-related ones like ecumenism or catechetics, or social situations like unemployment or marriage problems, the Irish Churches can learn from experiences elsewhere. When dealing with Northern Ireland, however, we are forced back on our own resources. Any solutions or new perspectives must come from ourselves. For this reason also the problems of Northern Ireland pose a fundamental challenge to Christian faith as it is lived and understood in Ireland.

Since we are dealing primarily with Irish Catholicism our examination of the challenge of Northern Ireland will focus primarily on the Catholic Church. However, though caught on different sides of the political or 'tribal' divide, the challenge to all Churches and the ways they responded to that challenge have been broadly similar. Thus an examination of the Catholic Church can serve broadly to represent the situation of all the main Churches.

The first aspect of the challenge posed by the Northern Ireland situation to the Catholic Church which must be examined is one which the Church itself has largely ignored. This is the challenge to its own institutional power. Only when it can be seen to what extent the Church itself felt threatened by the emerging civil rights movement in the late 1960s can we begin to understand the nature of the response it began to make in its attempts to contribute towards a settlement of the problem. An assessment of the various responses made by the Church leads us to look again at the roots of the problem and suggest some key areas where the Church could make a stronger response.

INSTITUTION UNDER THREAT

Though largely coming from the Catholic side of the 'tribal' divide and championing reform on housing, voting rights, and the police which would almost exclusively have benefited Catholics, elements in the programme of the Civil Rights Association also ran directly counter to the cherished values of many Catholic clergy. This was true particularly of its emphasis on the need to desegregate schooling allowing Catholic and Protestant children to be educated together rather than in separate schools. This issue continues to be a highly emotive one not just for most Catholic clergy but many lay people also and its inclusion among the reforms demanded by the civil rights movement was not calculated to win the support of the clergy. Similarly its stress on the need for reform in such areas as the availability of contraception and divorce in the Republic alienated many clergy.

For the highly conservative leadership in the diocese of Down and Connor, in which Belfast lies, the political changes which began to follow in the wake of the new British and international interest in Northern Ireland weakened the Church's control over Catholic politicians. In the years of Protestant dominance from the foundation of the northern state in 1921 the Catholic Church

had developed close links with the nationalist party, the traditional party representing Catholic interests until the SDLP was
founded in 1970. Parish priests often chaired the party's conven-
tions to select parliamentary candidates and Church leaders often
discussed with nationalist party representatives how they should
vote on particular issues.

The founding of the SDLP symbolised the coming to the fore
of a new breed of younger and more progressive Catholic politicians little inclined to take political direction from the Church.
With the political situation apparently moving out of its control
in the early 1970s, therefore, Church leaders in Belfast sought to
ensure an element of clerical control over many of the groups
emerging in Catholic areas in response to the troubles. It was
true, in particular, with regard to the citizens' defence committees,
set up by the people to help defend their areas against Protestant
mobs. Fr Des Wilson remembers attending a meeting at Bishop
Philbin's house at which the priests present were told to take over
these new committees. The Central Citizens Defence Committee,
founded in late 1969 to coordinate the activities of the different
local committees, was given a premises by the Church
to meet in and a conservative Catholic businessman,
became its chairman and led the organisation together with a
local priest.

For many of the ordinary people in the Catholic ghettos in
those early violent years their Church appeared to let them down
in their hour of need. This was graphically symbolised by the
presence of Bishop Philbin urging the people to take down the
barricades they had erected as their only defence against mobs
attacking their homes. Not only was the bishop unsuccessful but
the open opposition to him by middle-aged women who came
out to argue against him showed that when it came to political
issues they saw the Church as being against them. This was further
underlined for these Catholics when they saw the army being
given the use of Church schools during Operation Motorman in
July 1972 to clear the 'no-go' areas in Belfast and Derry.

As the British army was used more and more against Catholics
few priests spoke out about the harassment being experienced

by the people. According to Fr Des Wilson the clergy were more worried about preventing the rise of any republican or left-wing movements than about defending the people. The issues which dominated priests' meetings in those years, he says, concerned Mass and vestments and not the plight of the Catholic people. The few priests who tried to raise these issues and get the clergy to respond in some way found more opposition than support from the Church leadership and many left the priesthood or went elsewhere to work outside the north. The experience of Fr Wilson himself is a sign of the dilemma in which these priests found themselves. His attempts to respond to the needs of the people as a curate in Ballymurphy through trying to foster new forms of popular education got no support from his own parish priest, he says, and when he asked for permission to move into a council house to be closer to the people he was refused. Forced to choose, therefore, between loyalty to the Church institution or commitment to the people he chose to remain close to the people but to do so he had formally to adopt the status of a retired priest in 1975. Even then, when he moved into the council house he had wanted to occupy as curate, Church authorities put pressure on Belfast City Council to have the house taken from him. One of Bishop Cahal Daly's first moves in taking over as bishop in late 1982 was to accept Fr Wilson back into the diocese but he has chosen to remain working in the popular education programme he developed in Ballymurphy.

Due to the role it played during those crucial years, therefore, the Catholic Church has lost credibility among the ordinary Catholic people. This has added to a decline in Church-going which had already begun before the troubles broke out. It is now thought that only around 40% go to Church regularly in working class areas of Belfast. But, perhaps more significantly, it also indicates the reason why the continuous calls by Church leaders for an end to violence have little or no effect among these people. Paradoxically it is even now being argued that the support for the SDLP by Church leaders like Bishop Cahal Daly may be damaging that party in the polls since the bishop has been so vocal in his condemnation of Sinn Féin and the Provisional IRA.

While there are many complex reasons for the growth in electoral support for Sinn Féin it is by now obvious that the Church's influence over the political options exercised by Catholics is extremely limited.

EFFORTS TO RESPOND

In their submission to the New Ireland Forum in January 1984, the bishops stated that 'Ireland is one of the most ecumenically active countries in the world at the moment'. While it is a difficult statement to substantiate the numerous ecumenical initiatives listed in the submission indicate that this has been the most notable response by the Churches to the Northern Ireland troubles. At leadership level the leaders of the four main Churches have, since 1969, regularly met together and issued common appeals for an end to violence and for reconciliation among the communities. In December 1974 they launched their own peace campaign.

Out of these meetings grew the Joint Group on Social Questions with representatives of the Catholic Church and the Irish Council of Churches which acts as an advisory group to the Churches on social issues. Among the studies completed have been ones on drug abuse, housing in Northern Ireland, teenage drinking and rural underdevelopment. Undoubtedly their most important report was the one entitled *Violence in Ireland,* issued in 1976, which made concrete recommendations to the Churches on steps to be taken to achieve peace and reconciliation. Meetings such as the Ballymascanlon conferences held roughly every two years since 1973 between leading members of the main Churches, the annual Greenhills and Glenstal conferences and numerous other informal meetings bring Church leaders together regularly. One concrete fruit of these meetings was the establishment of an Inter-Church Emergency Fund in 1974 giving grants to local projects working for reconciliation. The money for this fund comes from Protestant and Catholic Churches in Europe.

At grass-roots level this activity has been mirrored in a whole network of ecumenical and peace groups which have grown up, particularly in Northern Ireland. These take the form of prayer or bible study groups, ecumenical groups like PACE (Protestant and Catholic Encounter), or local peace committees and 'fraternals' where the local clergy of different Churches meet regularly together. Among the best known of these groups was the Peace People, established in 1976 and later awarded the Nobel Peace Prize. Various ecumenical communities have also been established like Corrymeela which sponsors conferences and study groups in its residential centre outside Ballycastle, Cornerstone community on the Springfield Road between Catholic and Protestant ghettos in Belfast, the Columbanus Community of Reconciliation also in Belfast, and communities like Dismas House in Belfast and Columba House in Derry for the care of ex-prisoners.

Apart from these ecumenically-based ventures, Catholic Church leaders themselves have taken a coherent stand against paramilitary violence while also acknowledging the injustice and oppression suffered by ordinary Catholics and calling for meaningful reforms. In numerous and repeated statements year after year since the troubles began the Catholic bishops of the province have re-iterated this position. Even though it is sometimes argued that Cardinal Ó Fiaich is more sympathetic to Sinn Féin than, for example, is Bishop Cahal Daly, such differences are only ones of slight emphasis and often arise from the different circumstances of their two dioceses. Overall the bishops have spoken with a very unified voice. Representations have been made regularly to the authorities on particular issues most notably on the republican hunger-strike in the Maze prison in late 1980 and most of 1981. Both Cardinal Ó Fiaich and Bishop Edward Daly of Derry urged concessions on the key issues, of prison clothing and work, in numerous meetings with ministers but were disappointed by the rigid stance of the government.

Pope John Paul II sent his personal secretary, the Northern Ireland priest, Monsignor John Magee, to visit Bobby Sands in an unsuccessful effort to persuade him to end his fast. The Irish Justice and Peace Commission, an official commission of the Catholic bishops' conference, was involved in talks with the Northern Ireland minister in charge of prisons, Mr Michael

Alison, and in June 1981 it issued a detailed proposal on prison clothes, association and work which, it was hoped, could be the basis for a settlement. While all these initiatives failed to find a way out of the impasse, Fr Denis Faul, a prison chaplain in the Maze prison/Long Kesh, did, through his meetings with relatives of the hunger-strikers, exercise indirect pressure for an end to the protest. Fr Faul has, together with Fr Raymond Murray, a chaplain to the women's prison in Armagh, been active in publicising cases of ill-treatment of people held in detention by the security forces. Considered close to the republican politics of Sinn Féin by some critics, he has condemned the violent campaign of the Provisional IRA and the INLA in strong terms on numerous occasions.

However, the impact of these activities on the deeply polarised Catholic and Protestant working class communities and the different forms of violence resulting from their aspirations and fears – from that of the paramilitaries to the sectarian violence perpetrated by members of the security forces – has been minimal. Most of the ecumenical activity has been confined to small middle-class groups and too often rests content with merely facilitating friendly contacts between Protestants and Catholics. The deep-rooted political divisions between the communities are mostly avoided in such activities.

Even the important and far-reaching proposals of the officially sponsored working party which drew up the report *Violence in Ireland* have been largely neglected in practice. Though the Catholic bishops did respond positively to the report in a statement in 1977, the principal result has been the setting up of a joint programme for peace education in about 600 schools, north and south of the border. Little appears to have been done about the far more substantial proposal recommending the establishment of a Christian Centre of Social Investigation to investigate problems underlying social unrest or that recommending the Churches to set an example to society in the place they give to women in the life of the Church. It is only since Bishop Daly moved to Belfast that impetus has been given to implement the recommendation for closer contact between Catholic and Protestant schools. It is more difficult to monitor with what success proposals have been implemented on encouraging interdenominational youth activities, the education of Church members in the political and social implications of Christian faith or the suggestion that political leaders be encouraged to see their task as securing a just agreement with their opponents rather than in achieving victory over them. But on these also little of substance appears to have been done.

Ultimately, however, as the bishops themselves acknowledged in their submission to the Forum, Church leaders have failed to secure their overall objective of a just and lasting peace. Indeed they went on to admit: 'Perhaps we should all have realised earlier that the power of the Churches to provide solutions in this field is strictly limited.' Not only do they acknowledge failure in what they have done, therefore, but they even admit that almost anything they could do would fail. Is this not an answer to Fr Enda McDonagh's question quoted at the beginning of this chapter? After a decade and a half of ever more polarised community divisions in Northern Ireland, are the Churches being forced to acknowledge that they are no longer a saving force in Irish society?

A QUESTION OF IDENTITY

Fundamentally the problem of Northern Ireland appears to be one of identity. Two opposed communities cling staunchly to historical identities which they feel are under threat. For the Protestants the threat comes not just from the IRA but from Dublin and London also. Thus they defiantly shout 'No Surrender' and refuse to admit any past faults on their part particularly in relation to the discrimination against Catholics. The religious manifestation of such an outlook is deeply fundamentalist, clinging to their simple conservative faith and defending it against what they see as the threats of ecumenism and Catholicism.

But on the Catholic side also such a threatened identity exists. They feel threatened by Protestant supremacy, by the security forces and particularly when coalition governments are in power, by Dublin. Their religious outlook also bears traces of a type of Catholic fundamentalism, clinging to those elements which appear essential to preserving the purity of their distinctive identity. For Catholics in Northern Ireland two issues in particular embody this threat – desegregated education and mixed marriages. Being educated in mixed schools with Protestants or having a member of one community marrying someone from the other side is perceived as a certain betrayal. For this reason an attitude of 'No Surrender' exists among Catholics on these two issues.

At an official level the Catholic Church has shown a similar attitude. In their submission to the Forum, the Catholic bishops made a persuasive defence of Catholic schooling in Northern Ireland arguing both that it did not contribute to community divisions and also that most Catholics would not want mixed schools. On mixed marriages the bishops issued a long-awaited directory in November 1983 which deeply disappointed Protestant Church leaders because it did not appear to them to embody any substantial change of traditional Catholic demands for the children of such a marriage to be brought up as Catholics. What matters on both these issues is that Catholic Church leaders, instead of seeking to challenge the sense of threatened identity among Catholics actually serve strongly to re-inforce it by their policy. They betray an attitude which indicates that they too remain victims of this historical identity instead of leaders who could seek to move with the people to fashioning a new identity.

Nowhere can it be more clear than in Northern Ireland that true identity can never be established by clinging to historical symbols and understandings. For just as every individual has to forge his or her own identity through the struggle to embody values and aspirations in the concrete circumstances of life and society, so too have communities to do the same. For any community, politics is the principal activity through which their identity is forged. This involves not just party political activity but all activity directed to creating a more just and vital community life. This process of creating new identities responding to the real needs of people today, particularly the real needs of the deprived, has been frozen in Northern Ireland for generations as two communities with a threatened sense of identity confront each other. For all their goodwill and attempts to contribute to a solution, the Churches have largely ignored this dimension. Politics itself has become a dirty word for Churchmen to be replaced by the term 'reconciliation' usually used in a very vague sense to mean general goodwill.

Instead of trying to bring two mutually exclusive identities together, therefore, Church leaders should be trying to facilitate people on both sides of the sectarian divide to fashion a new identity through the active process of fashioning new responses to their immediate community problems. This would demand sponsoring people in concrete self-help projects at grass-roots level – co-operatives, centres of popular education and culture, simple local services. As Fr Des Wilson has shown in Ballymurphy this process can lead the people to a new form of faith reflection on their own lives and activities, discovering in the process of helping themselves and building their own community a new and more vital faith. Bishop Cahal Daly may now be acknowledging this in his emphasis on the need for 'an option for the poor' but few of his priests are adequately prepared to make such an option.

The Northern Ireland problem is but the most glaring sign of the failure of the particular type of Church and understanding of Christianity which we have inherited to offer us any real resources with which to build a new future together. It is the final result of two Church traditions which grew so institutionalised and entrenched in defending themselves and their particular political outlooks that they became unable to offer a hope for the future. The nineteenth century was the crucial period when this happened. To this we must now turn.

READING

Cahal B. Daly, *Peace: The Work of Justice*. Veritas, Dublin, 1979.
Enda McDonagh, 'Ireland's Divided Disciples', in *The Furrow*, January 1982.
    The same issue contains a number of excellent articles on the

Northern Ireland problem from a Christian point of view.

Violence in Ireland: A Report to the Churches, Veritas, Dublin and Christian Journals, Belfast, 1976.

5. Imprisoning Catholicism

The Irish Catholic Church, as we know it today, is only just over one hundred years old. The Church which cautiously emerged from the era of the penal laws at the end of the eighteenth century would be hardly recognisable as a Catholic Church to most Irish people today. The faith which lived on among the people was strong but it showed itself remarkably resistant to the attempts by Church leaders to bring it under their control and mould it to their liking. Bishops' reports in this period show continuing concern at such enduring practices as wakes, pilgrimages to the shrines of local saints which they seemed to consider as occasions for faction fighting and drunkenness, agrarian secret societies and clandestine marriages. Despite episcopal worries many of the ordinary clergy seemed to accept such practices and at times actively enjoy them. Furthermore the religious beliefs of the people appear to have been very orthodox except for some harmless superstitions, or pisheogs as we would call them.

At an institutional level the Church was weak. Church-going was much lower than now: in Dublin, Cork, Belfast and Limerick between fifty and seventy-five per cent but in rural areas dropping much lower, probably being only around 25% in some places. Most parish churches were poor buildings with little decoration. The numbers of clergy, though increasing up until the Famine in 1845, were in no way keeping up with the increase in the population in that period and the ratio of priests to people had dropped from 1:1,587 in 1731 down to 1:2,996 by 1840. The clergy wore no distinctive clerical dress to mark them off from the people and bishops like Archbishop Murray of Dublin (1823-52) or Bishop Doyle of Kildare and Leighlin (1819-34) discouraged the display of Catholic emblems like crucifixes or rosary beads in public. The Catholic network of schools, hospitals and other charitable institutions, that we take for granted, was almost completely non-existent. There were only a handful of nuns in Ireland in 1800 and less than 400 male religious, a figure which was fast declining. The devotional practices which we regard as so characteristic of Irish Catholicism, from the Sacred Heart novenas to Benediction, were only beginning to be introduced and would take decades before becoming popular.

From being essentially a folk church, therefore, the last century has witnessed the moulding of Irish Catholicism into a formidable and powerful institution, under the control of a fast-expanding body of clergy and religious who proved themselves extremely disciplined and obedient. Presiding over this institution was a group of bishops who, as the century wore on, became ever more publicly united and loyal to Rome. For the ordinary lay Catholic, whose life was touched more and more by this expanding network of institutions, what was offered was a variety of new and emotionally satisfying devotions. It is these three elements, institutionalism, clericalism and devotionalism which lie at the heart of the crisis of the Irish Catholic Church today.

AN EXPANDING INSTITUTION

The nineteenth century was the great age of church building in Ireland. Most of our Catholic parish churches date back to that period. By the 1860s there were 2,339 churches in the country, 2,000 of which had been built since the beginning of the century. Sometimes this involved building a finer building on the site of a former one that had been used as a Mass centre and in some cases even the second building was replaced in time with a yet more elaborate one. This was particularly true in the towns where an expanding and prosperous Catholic middle class donated much wealth to the Church.

But even more striking than the new network of churches was the growth of a network of Catholic schools, hospitals and charitable institutions. This was made possible because of the phenomenal growth of religious orders, both male and female, which began around the turn of the last century and lasted up until the mid 1960s. It was most marked in the case of nuns. In 1771 the Ursulines were brought to Cork by Nano Nagle to open a Catholic secondary school for the girls of wealthy families and four years later this was complemented by her foundation of the Presentation sisters to teach the poor. The latter in particular expanded rapidly opening their first school in Dublin in George's Hill in 1794. Numerous other Irish orders followed: in 1816 the Irish Sisters of Charity were founded by Mary Aikenhead to nurse and care for the poor and in 1835 they founded St Vincent's Hospital in Dublin, the first Catholic hospital in the country since the reformation. Catherine McAuley founded the Sisters of Mercy in the 1820s in the face of staunch clerical opposition. By 1851 there were 1,160 nuns in the country but it was in the aftermath of the Famine that the major growth in numbers took place reaching 8,031 by 1901 and continuing up to a peak of 15,145 in 1970.

With the foundation of the Christian Brothers by Edmund Rice in Waterford in 1802 and the establishment of the Presentation Brothers by a breakaway group in Cork in 1826, a similar network of Catholic schools for boys began to develop. While the brothers concentrated on the education of the poor, the establishment of Clongowes by the Jesuits in 1814 and Castleknock by the Vincentians in 1832 together with the growing number of diocesan colleges which, by 1820, were functioning in Navan, Waterford, Tullow, Ballaghadereen, Mountrath, Tuam and Waterford met the needs of the expanding Catholic middle class. Again it was in the immediate post-Famine period that the great growth took place in secondary schools. These roughly trebled in number between 1845 and 1880.

To staff this expanding institutional Church new seminaries had already been established, at Carlow and Kilkenny in 1793 and Maynooth in 1795. Part of the inspiration for this came from a British government fearful of seeing Ireland's Catholic clergy, then trained exclusively in colleges on the continent, radicalised by the ideas of the French revolution. The seminaries could not, however, train enough priests to meet the needs of a fast-expanding population in the years immediately before the Famine and, apart from Maynooth and Carlow, none of the colleges provided adequate courses. Though Maynooth trained about half of the priests being ordained in the 1820s, numerous others were ordained with insufficient training and some continued to go abroad to seminaries. Again it was only at the time of the Famine that Maynooth began to expand (due to a much-increased grant from the British government in 1845) and this, coupled with the decline in the overall population of the country, allowed for the possibility of training enough priests to staff the expanding institutions. The number of diocesan priests increased steadily therefore, from 2,183 in 1840 to 2,527 in 1861 and by 1901 it was up to 2,938. This increase continued up to a peak of 4,054 in 1972 and has begun to decline since.

This network of institutions was established just in time to cater for the needs of the emigrant Irish Catholics in the post-Famine period. Apart from many of the Irish seminaries which trained priests to work with Irish emigrants throughout the English-speaking world, All Hallows College had been founded in 1842 for the express purpose of training diocesan priests to work abroad. Therefore, apart from the emigrant Irish taking their faith to Britain, the United States, South Africa and Australia, the institutions of the Catholic Church in these countries were established largely through the work of Irish clergy. Just as the Church was beginning to take on a definite institutional ethos at home, it began to export this same type of Church throughout the English-speaking world.

CLERICALISM

One of the constant pre-occupations of Irish bishops in the early part of the last century was to impose discipline on their priests. This was not due to any great scandals associated with the lifestyle of most priests; the most frequent problem referred to in bishops' reports is a clerical fondness for drink, a vice far from eradicated to this day. Rather bishops sought to regulate the lives of their priests, ensuring, for example, that they preached regularly, celebrated the sacraments with decorum and attended annual theological conferences and retreats. They sought to restrict the amount of land that could be held by a priest to ensure that he was devoting himself full-time to his ministry. Many of these reforms, contained in the decrees of numerous diocesan synods up and down the country in the early decades of the century, were laudable. But they also served to enforce a greater distance between the priest and his people through enforcing the wearing of clerical dress and forbidding clerical attendance at such places as pubs, dances, race-meetings or theatres.

Another vexed question which kept recurring from the beginning of the 1820s with O'Connell's organisation of the Catholic people as a political force, was the issue of the involvement of priests in politics. From the beginning O'Connell's success depended on priests organising their people to counter the influence of the local landlord. Such an involvement, to ensure the election of a candidate favourable to Catholic interests, was quite acceptable to bishops, many of whom themselves openly supported such candidates. As the century wore on, however, many bishops did seek to limit the more active involvement of priests. A synod in Leinster in 1831, in forbidding both the use of churches for public meetings of the laity and the proclamation from the altar of any announcement except reading the banns of marriage, was setting its face against using the church for political purposes. Equally, at times when violent rebellion was a political issue, bishops remained very cautious. Cardinal Cullen, the dominant figure in the hierarchy from his appointment as Archbishop of Armagh in 1849 from where he moved to become Archbishop of Dublin in 1852, made the most strenuous attempts at Rome to have Archbishop MacHale of Tuam (1834-81) censured for protecting a priest of his diocese, Fr Lavelle, who continued to write and speak publicly in favour of the violent overthrow of the government during the rise of the Fenians in the early 1860s. By the 1870s, however, partly because of the stronger organisation of the Irish party at Westminster and also due to the introduction of the secret ballot, the influence of priests at local level lessened though most remained sympathetic to a broadly nationalist outlook.

But in enforcing a strongly disciplined clerical control of the Church, the most important factor was the moulding of the bishops into a body that, publicly at least, could be seen to have a unified pastoral approach and to speak with one voice on major issues. At the beginning of the last century the bishops did not even meet as a body and many jealously guarded their local autonomy. Thus in some dioceses, even the decrees of the Catholic Church's Council of Trent (1545-63) had not been promulgated. Bishops took up openly opposed positions on all major public issues and, as instanced by the disagreement between Cardinal Cullen and Archbishop MacHale over Fr Lavelle, had deep and even bitter disagreements in public. Senior bishops in that earlier period, such as Archbishop Murray of Dublin (1823-52), Bishop Doyle of Kildare and Leighlin (1819-34) and Bishop Higgins of Ardagh (1829-53), some of the leading bishops of their time, held what were called gallican views on the papacy meaning that they would only obey papal directives under certain conditions.

Paul Cullen, who returned to Ireland as Archbishop of Armagh after eighteen years as rector of the Irish College in Rome, sought to strengthen the unity and discipline of the Irish hierarchy. He organised the first national synod of the Irish Church in 700 years which took place at Thurles in 1850 and in putting its seal on many of the local reforms introduced by bishops in the previous half decade, it imposed agreed measures of consultation on the bishops to avoid open squabbles. At a time when American bishops were adopting some parliamentary rules of deliberation for their meetings Cullen imposed an autocratic stamp on the deliberations of the Irish bishops which is maintained to this day and during his long period as Archbishop of Dublin up to 1878 he managed to have appointed as bishops men whom he could control and who would be little inclined to disagree with him.

Though Cullen himself could disagree with Rome and maintained his support for the separation of church and state even when it was condemned by Pope Pius IX in 1864, he did set his face firmly against any gallican tendencies in the Irish Church. Professor Crolly of Maynooth was forced to sign 'a most humble submission' in 1855 withdrawing such views and Cullen brought the Irish Catholic Church as a whole into obedient submission to Rome.

The nineteenth century, therefore, saw the clergy and their bishops united and disciplined in a way they never had been before but it was at the expense of their close identification with the people. Though they continued to identify with many popular aspirations, they did so as a distinct and identifiable group set apart from the people. They were held in a strong if somewhat exaggerated popular respect often tinged with fear but they met far too little of the criticism they had been subjected to in earlier periods. The Irish clergy came to resemble an efficient and well marshalled civil service administering and defending a powerful institution.

THE DEVOTIONAL REVOLUTION

The place assigned to the majority of Irish Catholics in this system was definitely one of submission. The laity were provided with a growing set of devotional practices introduced from Britain and the continent such as First Fridays, novenas to the Sacred Heart, exposition and benediction of the Blessed Sacrament, Forty Hours devotion and different forms of Marian devotion. These began to be introduced in the towns in the early part of the century but took many decades to spread around the country and achieve widespread popularity. This was accompanied by the spread of devotional books such as *The Lamp of the Soul* or *The Key of Heaven,* many of them from Britain, designed to instruct Catholics in a sentimental and individual piety.

These devotions were spread through parish missions, intro-duced by the Vincentians who conducted the first one at Athy in 1842, and soon taken up by other religious orders. These served not only to spread the new forms of devotion but also to strengthen the parish system throughout the country. Rates of Mass-going began to increase particularly in the post-Famine period when the growing numbers of churches could better cater for a declining population. At the same time the traditional prac-tice of celebrating Mass and confession in people's homes was abolished as much as possible; one of the decrees of the Synod of Thurles addressed itself to this. More and more, therefore, the people's religious practices took place in church and depended on clergy. However, the Church made no attempt to educate its laity in theology and thus its strong devotional fare contrasted with a great lack of solid intellectual training in the faith. Paradoxically as nationalist sentiment was growing in the country most people were being introduced to a devotional life derived from English Victorian piety and puritanism.

If traditional Irish spirituality suffered in this process so did ecumenism. Many Irish Catholic leaders of the early years of the century were remarkably ecumenical even by the standards of today. Bishop Doyle of Kildare and Leighlin put forward a scheme for the re-unification of the Catholic and Anglican Churches, offering to resign his See if it helped in the process. But the Protestant crusade of the 1820s to the 1870s put the Catholic Church on the defensive and, in a bid to protect its flock from the influence of aggressive Protestant missionaries, it began to emphasise the distinctively Catholic elements of this faith. Neither did Cardinal Cullen have much sympathy for Protestantism and in a celebrated dispute with the Church of Ireland Archbishop of Dublin, Richard Wately (1831-63), the latter had to withdraw texts he had written for the Board of National Education after Cullen had called them heretical.

'AN EXCLUDING CHURCH'

The Catholic Church which emerged in the last century was strongly popular. With the loss of the Irish language it became the single most important mark of our separate identity and as the century progressed being Catholic came to be synonymous in most people's minds with being Irish. That this newly-found national identity excluded a quarter of the island's people, the Protestants, appeared to worry few Church leaders. The bitter legacy of this was not to become apparent until the partition of the country in 1920.

Despite being popular, however, it was undoubtedly a narrow and illiberal version of Catholicism which became so successfully institutionalised. It has become fashionable in recent years to blame Cardinal Cullen for this development but set in the context of the papacy of Pope Pius IX (1846-78) it is remarkable that the Irish Church remained so open and sympathetic to the nationalist aspirations of the people. For the ultramontane movement, led by that Pope, increasingly centralised the Church under his control as symbolised by the definition of papal infallibility in 1870 and set its face solidly against any of the secular developments taking place in the Europe of the time.

Far more important than Cullen in ensuring the success of his highly institutionalised Church was the Famine. If that had not occurred the Church would have developed its many institutions but they could never have hoped to cater for the needs of the whole population. It is also doubtful whether, without the peculiar social patterns of post-Famine Ireland already referred to in Chapter One, there would have been as phenomenal an increase in vocations as there was. But, most importantly, the Famine helped to kill off the religious traditions of the people which, particularly in the countryside, provided an alternative popular culture which could never have been brought as successfully under clerical control. This is what the historian, Dr S. J. Connolly, is referring to when he closes his study *Priests and People in Pre-Famine Ireland 1780-1845* with the ominous words: '. . . when Irish Catholicism came into its inheritance it did so only by means of the destruction of a rival world.' The continuing existence of such a 'rival world' of popular traditions, even in an undoubtedly weakened form, might have helped to modify some of the worst intolerance, authoritarianism and clerical dominance within the Irish Catholic Church.

There was no possibility in the historical conditions of the last century that a different model of Church might have emerged in Ireland in the way, for example, that we see the folk Catholicism of Latin America today giving rise to a new popular model of Church. But without a Cullen some of the clergy might have resisted more successfully the total institutionalisation and centralisation of the Church and thus responded more sensitively to the people's needs. The remarkable championing of women's rights and exposure of the injustice of landlordism conducted so trenchantly in her many books and writings in the 1870s and 1880s by the famous Nun of Kenmare from her enclosed Poor

Clare convent is an example of such a prophetic response. But the growing clerical opposition which forced her to leave Ireland and eventually, before her death, to leave the Catholic Church showed just how dominant the needs of the institution had become, completely denying any more prophetic understanding of, and response to, the gospel.

In many ways it is the very success of the institutional Catholic Church in Ireland which is now its greatest weakness. In the words of a report compiled on the attitudes of young people to the Church in September 1983, young people see it as an 'excluding church', with most clergy and religious imprisoned in their institutions. For many of the priests and sisters aware of the crisis of faith, these institutions they have inherited are burdens prohibiting them from moving out and living among the people to fashion new ministries. But for numerous others the institutions have so completely cut them off from the people that they remain largely satisfied with a traditional understanding of their role. And, for the ordinary Irish lay Catholics, this institutional Church perpetuates a cycle of activities which, far from embodying any liberating dimension for their lives, simply adds another routine which they fulfil either out of duty or out of a belief in benefits it may bring. This, ultimately, is the tragedy of the Irish Catholic Church.

READING

S. J. Connolly, *Priests and People in Pre-Famine Ireland 1780-1845.* Gill and Macmillan, Dublin, 1982.

Desmond Keenan, *The Catholic Church in Nineteenth-Century Ireland: A Sociological Survey.* Gill and Macmillan, Dublin, 1983.

Desmond Bowen, *Paul Cardinal Cullen and the Shaping of Modern Irish Catholicism.* Gill and Macmillan, Dublin, 1983.

Patrick J. Corish, *The Catholic Community in the Seventeenth and Eighteenth Centuries.* Helicon, Dublin, 1981.

6. Resources for an Irish Spirituality

As the last century progressed, the principal pre-occupation of Irish Church leaders became the creation of an efficient and disciplined Church organisation. Though they were at times scandalised by some of the traditional Christian practices of the people, such as the confession of women in people's houses on the occasion of station Masses, Church leaders never had to doubt the fact that Irish Catholics were wholeheartedly a believing people. Throughout the fourteen hundred years of Irish Christianity the Church had been predominantly a people's Church. Our identification of the Church with institutions and clergy would have puzzled our ancestors. Instead, for them, the Church was the *pobal Dé,* the people of God, and the church building was the *teach an phobail,* the people's house. Even the early Irish monasteries were known as households, *muintir,* rather than as institutions.

The most crucial fact about the Irish Catholic Church today is that this intimate link between faith and people has been profoundly weakened. For the younger, more educated urban dwellers identified in Chapter Three we can say that this link has been broken. Irish Church leaders today therefore face a situation which is the direct opposite to that faced by their predecessors in the last century. If anything, our Church institutions are far too efficient and disciplined thus channelling the people's faith and its forms of expression in the safe ways a conservative clergy find easy to manage. Though few Irish clergy seem willing to acknowledge it, the task of the Church today is to forge again a spirituality expressive of the Irish experience and one which can make a vital contribution to the growth of a new humanism in Ireland. For, as Pope Paul VI said in his encyclical, *Populorum Progressio* (1967), the Church must share 'the noblest aspirations of men and women and. . . wishes to help them attain their full flowering'.

In undertaking such a task, Irish Christians have available

to them a rich tradition of native spirituality, far richer than that available to Christians in most parts of the world. But the temptation of simply re-creating some of the practices of our ancestors must be avoided. Such would be a death-wish since we cannot, and should not, want to re-create the kind of society and culture they lived in. Rather the challenge for us must be to re-appropriate the more Christian elements of our ancestors' spirituality and find new ways to embody these for our times.

Undoubtedly one of the great tragedies of the Irish Catholic Church has been its neglect of, and at times open opposition to, the spirituality which Irish men and women forged in their struggles to live out the gospel amid the realities of their historical situation. Instead the Church, over the past century, facilitated the introduction of a new spirituality from the continent which was not only different from that of the Irish, but in many key ways taught an approach to God and the world which was the direct opposite of the Irish approach. Thus where the old was intimate with God and saw his hand in the things of the world, the new was stylised and sentimental encouraging a divorce between things spiritual and material. The new emphasised an individual approach to God and the legalistic fulfilment of duties where the old was deeply communitarian with a strong distaste for religious hypocrisy and mere outward practice. Even the elements of the old which survived, notably the regular saying of the rosary and penitential practices such as those at Croagh Pádraig and Lough Derg, came to be seen by many as ways to placate God rather then helping to develop a deep religious sense. Much of the rejection by young people today of what passes for Christian faith in Ireland is in fact the rejection of this more recent spirituality, or rather the decadent forms of it which are all many Irish Catholics have inherited. If many of these young people retain any openness to Christianity at all after their negative and repressive experiences of it, they would be surprised to find that a more authentic, gentle, tolerant and yet demanding faith was lived by their ancestors which had a deeply developed social conscience, a healthy anti-clericalism and a complete absence of puritanism and prudery when it came to sexual matters. The principal lessons it has to teach us can be grouped under three headings: religious sensitivity, community basis and social contribution.

RELIGIOUS SENSITIVITY

For our ancestors, God was not known through theoretical concepts nor through rarified experience but rather in the everyday familiar things of the world. God's presence was everywhere and because of this Christ and the principal saints, particularly Mary, were addressed with familiarity and intimacy. Even the more complex doctrines of the faith were translated by the Irish in a completely authentic way into the familiar and everyday. Where this is clearly seen is in the hundreds of folk prayers and poems handed on by the ordinary people themselves from generation to generation. Few cultures could have expressed the complex doctrine of the Trinity as well as these people did:

> Three folds in cloth, yet there is but the one cloth.
> Three joints in a finger, yet there is but the one finger.
> Three leaves in a shamrock, yet there is but the one shamrock.
> Frost, snow and ice. . . yet the three are only water.
> Three Persons in God likewise, and but the one God.

More recent generations of Irish would have been shocked by the intimate way their ancestors addressed God and the saints. The eighth century poet, Blathmac, called Jesus 'darling son of the virgin' and Mary 'little bright-necked one'. These familiar terms, which abound in Irish folk spirituality, lose much in translation but indicate a deeply developed sensitivity to the presence of the divine entirely missing from the more stylised and sentimental prayer forms current over the past hundred years. Inseparable from this sense of God was a deep sense of Christ and Mary present in the suffering and the poor. A common theme in Irish religious tales is the appearance of Christ as a poor beggar and Irish poets frequently linked the sufferings of the people to those of Christ on the cross and Mary at its foot.

In no way can this sense of the divine be seen as superstitious. Rather it was, from the very earliest centuries, deeply rooted in the scriptures. We get some glimpse of this from the scriptural representations on the ancient Irish high crosses which still remain and from the attention devoted to the lavish ornamentation of the bible by the early Irish monks. But, more importantly, the poems and stories which came down to us in the folk tradition show evidence also of being deeply scriptural and they never wander off into the embellished flights of fancy which some of our more recent spirituality is prone to especially when emphasising the passion of Christ or the life of Mary.

Irish scriptural scholarship in the early centuries was highly developed and drew on the different methods of interpretation current in both Alexandria and Antioch while the western Church at the time showed little interest in the latter. The 'three fifties', as the one hundred and fifty Psalms were called, were also the staple prayer of the Irish for many centuries. Sadly few Irish Catholics over the past century have had as deep a grounding in the bible as their ancestors had.

This spirituality was also critical of hypocrisy in prayer or mere outward attandance at Mass or confession. The folk tales portray such attendance as futile in comparison to which the earnest prayer of someone who misses Mass is of greater worth.

COMMUNITY BASIS

While our ancestors had a strong, personal sense of the all-pervasive presence of God, they saw none of the divisions that we do between one's individual relationship with God and its social expression, as if the former could exist without the latter. Hospitality, especially to the poor, was a deeply rooted religious value particularly since Christ was seen to be present in the poor person. It also appears that our common practice of treating the poor as second class citizens would have been frowned on by our ancestors who were more accustomed to giving the poor person the place of honour at the fireside. It is significant that the religious values which abound in the Irish folk tales are what we would regard as more social values – generosity, justice, honesty, respect for life. Failure to help the poor, defrauding people of what is their due, injustices committed against the poor and killing are vividly portrayed as meriting eternal punishment. Significantly also, prayer for oneself alone is known in Irish as *paidir ghann,* a mean prayer.

What we would call today a developed social conscience was, therefore, inseparable from the religious faith of our ancestors unlike the division between faith and life which has characterised the spirituality of the past hundred years. At best this recent spirituality cultivated a paternalistic attitude to the poor which, however, lacked any developed awareness of sins of injustice against them. The appalling contradiction which allowed Christians grossly to exploit the poor while thinking themselves charitable because they donated to charities would have found strong condemnation in the traditional spirituality. Yet such a contradiction co-exists easily with our current spirituality.

Underlying this more social understanding of the faith was the strongly communal nature of its expression from the first centuries after St Patrick. Irish Catholicism had always been based on a strong sense of solidarity among the people, whether in the distinctive form of monastic universities which were the centre of Irish Church life up to the 1100s or afterwards in such genuine community get-togethers as pattern days, pilgrimages or station Masses which became the main religious and social occasions for the people. This sense of community, called *muintearas* in Ireland, characterised all pre-industrial societies but it conditioned the Irish faith experience more deeply than it seems to have done elsewhere.

In the tradition of station Masses we have a practice which could have helped develop local and intimate communities similar to the basic Christian communities growing up in many part of the world. The parish was divided up into different station areas and Mass was said for the area in one of the houses every spring and autumn. Though it continues to live on in some western dioceses, this practice was opposed by Church authorities during the last century and eradicated throughout most of the country.

However, at a time when the structure of the parish is unable to cope with the need for it to be in some sense a genuine Christian community this tradition of the station Mass, and the communal experience of faith it expressed, could with value be applied in new ways. This is particularly true in large urban parishes where, far from being a community, the parish has become simply a provider of religious services for individuals and families.

If, for our ancestors, their Christian faith was a natural part of their cultural ethos, the place of the priest was far less dominant than it has become over the past hundred years. Clerical vices were a favourite butt of Irish poets down the centuries, especially clerical greed. Neither did the priest hold the same fearful moral power over the lives of the people that recent Irish literature shows he had in recent times. Numerous folk poems up to the last century indicate that the Irish were well able to make up their own minds when it came to morality; as one anonymous poet expressed it:

> No priest or friar will I believe
> that it's sin to couple in love.

Yet, for all that, the priest remained a natural and respected member of the community.

SOCIAL CONTRIBUTION

As the Church worldwide is searching for ways of contributing to the growth of a new and more just society, a return by the Irish Church to some of the emphases of traditional spirituality would have much to offer this search. Such a return, however, could only begin through an openness and respect on the part of Irish Christians to the secularised, and at times even anti-Christian, culture growing up in Ireland. Such an attitude would be following the example of the early Irish monks who, far from condemning the pre-Christian culture then flourishing in the country, preserved and christianised it and in some cases, as for example the easy availability of divorce right up to the final collapse of Gaelic society, even accepted what by our standards should have been unacceptable. Instead of trying to impose its version of the gospel on a people little interested in accepting it in its present form, the Irish Church must instead seek to identify those gospel values growing up in the new culture and develop a new, more broadly based and possibly far richer, understanding of the gospel on the basis of these.

At a social level one of the new insights developing, largely on the margin of the Church, concerns the need for a new civilisation of simple living if there is ever to be justice for the oppressed of the earth. For traditional Irish spirituality simple living and a lack of desire for the accumulation of goods was a major value. In fact far greater value was placed on sharing than on possessing. However, our more recent spirituality has largely neglected the gospel emphasis on simplicity and sharing. The proverbial saying from the early Irish Church, *eochair cirte comhroinn,* (the key to justice is distribution) deserves to be highlighted and emphasised with a least the same sense of urgency traditionally afforded sexual morality.

Alongside the search for a new civilisation is the development of forms of therapy helping individuals to reach an emotional and particularly a sexual maturity. Many of these individuals would identify the Church as a major contributor to their inhibitions and problems in this area. Any forging of a genuine Irish spirituality will have to devote much sensitive attention to the ways Christian spirituality has warped and repressed people's sexual and emotional lives. It will have to return to the understanding of an earlier era which was much more tolerant and forgiving of sexual transgressions; an era when, to quote from one Spanish observer in 1579, 'the people seem extremely affectionate to each other; for even the men salute one another with kisses and the women shew nothing loth to give hearty embraces in the streets.' By all accounts our ancestors were affectionate and openly expressive of that affection, a far more healthy state of affairs than the rather morbid and obsessive interest in sexual matters which has characterised the Church over the past one hundred years.

But while Irish spirituality was flexible and forgiving, it was also robust and ascetic. Accounts of the severe ascetical practices of the early Irish monks or the penances associated with Croagh Padraig and Lough Derg seem almost perverse to our ears. But these practices indicate an underlying passion to remain faithful to a deeply held conviction and faith. This extremism takes on an added importance in a society where subtle forces of advertising and media manipulation seek to convince us all the time that having goods, using them and consuming them are our overriding values while peace, justice, love and truth are quite secondary. Living as Christians in our age demands, however, a passionate commitment to such values and the struggle for justice and peace demands ever more effective methods of social protest. It is interesting that some of the penitential practices of the Irish monks were themselves taken from pre-Christian forms of social protest. So while fasting was seen as a penitential expression of love for Christ it was also used as a way of exerting moral pressure or gaining redress for a wrong done. St Patrick himself had fasted against a slave owner in order to gain redress for the oppressed. The power of such a tradition is seen, for example, in the enormously significant forms of peaceful protest being used by the women's peace camp outside the military base at Greenham Common in England where American cruise missiles were delivered in December 1983. Through their determined use of peaceful methods which have demanded great self-sacrifice from those involved, this protest has generated a level of public support no violent protest could achieve and its moral power has shaken the British government. While such forms of protest are happening on the margins or outside the Church, they indicate the potential for harnessing this ascetic tradition to the forms of social resistance which have become a major way to express the love of Christ in our time.

Appropriating the richness of our traditional spirituality has numerous other contributions to make. The respectful attitude it had towards nature would make us more sensitive to the ecological damage being done by technological civilisation to our environment. Its commitment at artistic excellence might help us to find some more adequate visual expressions of our religious outlook than the gaudy and ugly iconography which, unfortunately, still remains far too much with us. In the one area in which the Irish Church can be said to have re-discovered the vigour of an aspect of its earlier tradition, namely in its missionary outreach, we can now see the highly positive impact it is having on Church and society at home.

While it is an obvious temptation in any age of crisis and transition to idealise the riches of the past, it is difficult to deny the many attractive and beneficial aspects of our native traditions of spirituality. At a time when the dominant spirituality of Irish Catholicism is unable to meet the needs of a new generation and people are attracted to numerous new cults and movements offering what appears to be a more living spirituality, the Church can ill-afford to dismiss such a rich heritage. But perhaps even more important than any desire to compete with what seem to be its first serious competitors on the religious scene, the new cults, our spiritual traditions can help us confront the new social challenges facing us in Ireland. As the Churches of Latin America teach us only too well, the Christian response to the extreme forms of capitalist exploitation evident throughout the world today demands a spirituality strong enough to withstand brutal persecution. There is growing evidence in Ireland that if groups of Christians begin to fashion responses to counter the gross injustices appearing in our society they too will meet strong opposition from the privileged. If this ever happens it will indicate that Irish spirituality has again come alive.

READING

John J. Ó Ríordáin, *Irish Catholics: Tradition and Transition*. Veritas, Dublin, 1980.
Michael Maher, ed., *Irish Spirituality*, Veritas, Dublin, 1981.

7. The Demands of Liberation

'The glory of God is the human person fully alive,' said St Irenaeus, Bishop of Lyons from 177 to 200 and one of the fathers or great teachers of the early Church. Unfortunately, however, at various periods throughout its life the Christian Church has tended to forget this intimate link between faith in God and, what we would now call, human liberation. Not only is everything that degrades and oppresses humanity opposed to the will of God but the bible tells us that God is closest to those struggling to realise their humanity, struggling for liberation. Indeed, as the liberation theologians remind us, it was in the process of liberating the enslaved Jews from Egypt that God showed his face to them. Later in their history various prophets emerged to remind them that oppression of the poor was the greatest sin against God, pitting the oppressor directly against God who is on the side of the poor. In proclaiming what he called the kingdom of God, Jesus was also taking up the great hope of the Jewish poor for a new society of justice to be realised not just in heaven but on earth also. The God preached by the Church, therefore, not only condemns all injustice and oppression but is to be fully found among the poor and oppressed struggling for liberation. And the most essential promise of this God is that history is moving towards the fulfilment of the hope of the oppressed, the realisation of justice on earth.

In our times again the Church has become more fully aware that action for justice is an essential aspect of its mission to bring the gospel alive. The 1971 Synod of Bishops in Rome even went so far as to make effective action for justice the criterion for the credibility of the gospel today: 'Unless the Christian message of love and justice shows its effectiveness through action in the cause of justice in the world, it will only with difficulty gain credibility with the men and women of our times.' Similarly this emphasis on justice has come to dominate the social teaching of the Church, developed in new directions by Pope John XXIII, Pope Paul VI and now by Pope John Paul II. This new emphasis can be summed up by a stirring passage from the apostolic exhortation, *Evangelii Nuntiandi,* issued in December 1975 by Pope Paul VI. Referring to the millions of people throughout the world whose struggles had been articulated by their bishops at the 1974 Synod of Bishops, the Pope goes on: 'Peoples, as we know, engaged with all their energy in the effort and struggle to overcome everything which condemns them to remain on the margin of life: famine, chronic disease, illiteracy, poverty, injustices in international relations and especially in commercial exchanges, situations of economic and cultural neo-colonialism sometimes as cruel as the old political colonialism. The Church, as the bishops repeated, has the duty to proclaim the liberation of millions of human beings, many of whom are her own children – the duty of assisting the birth of this liberation, of giving witness to it, of ensuring it is complete. This is not foreign to evangelisation.'

These words, repeated and made his own by Pope John Paul II when opening the historic Puebla conference of Latin American bishops in Mexico in 1979, indicate not just a concern for the poor but a siding with them in their concrete struggles against the economic and social structures that oppress them. They also commit the Church to an understanding of liberation not content with simple reforms but demanding a complete and authentic liberation. It was in prophetic response to such words as these that the bishops of Latin America made their preferential option for the poor at Puebla, the single most important step taken by any sector of the leadership of the Catholic Church since the reformation, according to many theologians.

Conservative interests have reacted to these moves by proclaiming with ever greater insistence that religion should have nothing to do with politics. They seek a purely spiritualistic religion that will not threaten their privileged position, benefiting from the exploitation of the poor if not directly engaged in it. While some churchmen side with this view fearful of the changes taking place around them, the official teaching of the Catholic Church as well as the practice of numerous bishops and priests, including the Pope himself, makes it clear that conversion to gospel values cannot be limited to individuals but that new political, economic and social systems must be devised which can promise justice to the poor. Indeed Pope John Paul's insistence that priests should not take up positions in party politics has been consistently misquoted to imply that priests should not actively encourage their people to struggle for justice. But the example of the Pope himself, especially in the concrete support he has given workers in his native Poland, shows that for him Christianity demands not just individual but also social conversion. Essential to work for social conversion is opposing injustice, unmasking the ideology which underpins it and empowering the people to struggle against it.

OPPOSING INJUSTICE

Though the Irish Catholic Church has highlighted areas of injustice in our society and sought reforms, through documents such as the bishops' pastoral letter on justice in 1977 or the annual pre-budget submissions to the minister of finance made by the St Vincent de Paul Society, to name but two examples, such initiatives rarely seek the root cause of such injustice in order effectively to pinpoint the basic problem. This lack of a thorough political, economic and social analysis simply mirrors our society as a whole which has been very reluctant to uncover the new web of injustice which is an integral part of the type of economic and social development we have been following since the early 1960s.

At one level this development has proved very successful as shown, for example, by the first ever World Bank report in 1978 which placed Ireland among the top thirty industrialised countries. But if Ireland in the last twenty-five years has joined the rich elite of nations which dominate and distort for their own good the world economy, most Irish people are not benefiting from this privileged position. In one of the very few studies to have been done on the distribution of income in the Republic, a team from the Economic and Social Research Institute published a report in 1982 which highlighted the growing inequalities in Irish society: 'Ireland may enter the twenty-first century with an upper middle class so privileged and so securely entrenched as to harken back to its nineteenth century predecessors.'

Not only do government taxation policies fail to redistribute wealth effectively, the report found, but the domination by the wealthy elite of opportunities such as access to third-level education ensures that the rich grow richer while the poor get poorer. Though the value of social welfare payments has increased more than the rate of inflation so that people on social welfare are now slightly better off than they would have been in the 1960s, the value of wages has increased by more, so that social welfare recipients are worse off now relative to those on wages than they would have been in the 1960s. Furthermore the numbers depending on social welfare for an income has jumped from 18.6% of the population in 1966 to a massive 30% in 1975, a level which has remained fairly constant since then.

Resorting to international recession as an explanation for the growing gap between rich and poor in Ireland and particularly for the ever-higher levels of unemployment cannot excuse us from a more rigorous analysis. For even though the international recession has had an impact on our economy the basic flaw lies in the structure of that economy itself. As Fr Frank Sammon SJ pointed out in a detailed paper at the Kilkenny Poverty Conference in 1981 'the way in which we have been organised for growth has entailed a growing proportion of our population being considered.a liability: it has, in a sense, generated poverty.' This has happened because of the priority given by all governments in recent decades to paying massive sums of money (IR£2,800 million between 1973 and 1981, according to the Telesis report) to private companies, many of them giant multi-national companies, to generate jobs while demanding from them only very low levels of taxation. If it had succeeded the moral questionableness of a policy which expected those on average incomes to pay higher taxes so that the rich could be pampered to 'take risks' might have been overlooked. But it has been a dismal failure, succeeding in increasing total employment by only 26,000 between 1957 and 1980. If the best that could be done was just over 1,000 new jobs a year in the years of economic expansion in the 1960s then the outlook is bleak indeed in a period of economic decline and population growth in which, simply to return to the unemployment level of 1979, between 27,000 and 31,000 new jobs would have to be created by 1986. This dependence on multi-national companies means we have served their needs in the way we served the needs of the British economy during our long years as a British colony.

At the same Kilkenny conference, Mr Joe Holland, who works for the Jesuit Centre for Concern in Washington DC, put this new dependence on the multi-national companies in an international context. Their dominance of the world economy has taken power away from national governments who find that they are now competing with Third World countries where labour costs are very low. Thus they find they have to reduce labour costs at home and, as ever greater numbers are losing their jobs due to this competition, they can afford less and less social welfare payments. The whole phase of capitalism which dated from the Second World War during which governments protected the weaker sectors of their people, so-called social welfare capitalism, is now being replaced by a type of capitalism in which the multi-nationals replace people with machines to do the jobs. This is often referred to as 'a second industrial revolution', alerting us to the fact that its social effects are going to be every bit as dramatic as those that occurred during the industrial revolution of the last century. With no commitment either to their workforce or even to the city or town where they have set themselves up, the multi-national company will shut down overnight if bigger profits can be made elsewhere. The prospect facing us, therefore, is for ever higher unemployment and falling living standards.

Faced with this new form of capitalism, the Church finds itself in a very advantageous position, Mr Holland argues. Together with the trade union movement, the Church is the only other major social institution which seeks to bring people together in community and solidarity rather than in competition with each other. Furthermore the Church is a transnational organisation and it thus could play a major role in linking the struggles of the poor across national boundaries since the giant companies which exploit them operate also with no concern for national boundaries.

UNMASKING IDEOLOGY

If people could see clearly what was happening to the economy of the world under the impact of the multi-national companies they could demand some controls on them. But the success of these companies is to put forward a view of the world, an ideology, which makes people view them in a favourable light and blame workers, trade unions and the poor for their problems. The sophisticated advertising of these companies is the most obvious example of how this happens. But in a more concerted way they have helped foster a view of the world, enunciated by such leaders as President Reagan or Mrs Thatcher, which justifies a huge arms build-up – from which the multi-nationals that build the weapons profit – while cutting back social services and benefits to their own people. Attempts by countries to build new economic systems not under the control of the multi-nationals and seeking to distribute employment, wealth and opportunities to all and not just the privileged few, such as Nicaragua or Grenada before the American invasion in October 1983, find themselves ostracised and even under armed attack from powerful governments, particularly the United States.

Any view of the world which sees the poor as a threat while spending billions of pounds on armaments is directly opposed to the Christian gospel. This is why Christians and their Church in many parts of the world find themselves increasingly in open protest against their own governments. But such an ideology is very pervasive and deeply rooted and finds expression at many levels. It is not uncommon to find property owners in the suburbs of our cities and towns, for example, organising in opposition to the travelling people refusing to give them any stopping place near their own estates. Our police and army are built up more and more as a response to rising crime levels in place of any rigorous questioning of our economic and social policies which, because leading to such increases in unemployment and poverty, directly drive people to crime. Many of the rich even yet persist in blaming the laziness of the poor for their failure to find jobs, claiming they can earn more from unemployment benefit. Not only does this contradict the fact that the vast majority of people on such benefits only receive about a half of what they would get if working but it refuses to examine the deep-rooted structural problems of our economy and the bleak prospects ahead.

This view of the world, blaming the poor for the problems of our society and economy, must be unmasked by the Church if it is to make an option for the poor. This can happen at many levels. Firstly, the Church should sponsor rigorous analyses of the real causes of our problems and uncover the growing social inequalities which exist. Though this is to some extent being done, such analyses usually end up in densely written reports never accessible to the people themselves, particularly those who are directly suffering from the system and its ideology. A major step has been taken in this direction by the Jesuit Centre for Faith and Justice in Dublin in popularising the findings of recent studies on Irish society through seminars and publications.

But discovering and educating people about the true nature of our social situation is not enough. This must go hand-in-hand with a major effort by the Church to confront the people, particularly the wealthy and powerful, with the social effects of the policies they foster. Far more than helping the poor, the example of Jesus is one of confronting the rich and powerful, demanding that they change. Unfortunately the Irish Catholic Church has remained far too close to the rich and powerful in Irish life, educating their children and providing them with many other social services. As a wealthy property and landowner the Church also finds itself at times sharing the outlook and values of the rich. The contradictions inherent in this position were graphically pointed out by the then minister of state at the Department of the Environment, Mr Ruairi Quinn, TD, in a Seanad debate on the Homeless Persons Bill in November 1983. Welcoming a telex from the Conference of Major Religious Superiors in support of the bill, Mr Quinn went on to express the hope that these religious orders would facilitate the housing programmes of local authorities by selling them some of their extensive land holdings at their existing use value instead of selling them to private developers at the far higher prices these developers can offer. The record of the Church in this regard is very poor, Mr Quinn reminded the senators. In seeking to preach the gospel to the rich, therefore, not only must the Church refuse to water down its stark message of conversion to a simplicity of life and to the cause of the poor but it must also uproot itself from its deep institutional complicity in the unjust structures and values perpetuated by the rich to defend their own privilege.

In a reply to an attack on him by Dr Conor Cruise O'Brien, Monsignor Bruce Kent of British CND showed what such unmasking of ideology means in practice. Early on in his article (*The Observer,* 4 December 1983) Monsignor Kent pinpointed the ideology or 'gospel' as he called it, which Dr O'Brien was defending: 'Not that Dr O'Brien does actually lack a gospel for our society. We all have one. He enjoys his and defends it with vigour. It is not just pragmatic: it is one of power. It is a gospel of comfortable Western liberalism underpinned by a rather more uncomfortable, for some, Western capitalism.'

Monsignor Kent ends his article by showing up something of the reality of Western capitalism, what sin has done to his society as he says, and he does so from the standpoint of the poor: 'Prisoners, three in a cell in ancient prisons, sharing the same chamber pot while part-time directors clear their £45,000 a year. An arms trade now topping a billion pounds a year while millions in the Third World countries go hungry. Empty houses and luxury homes while the homeless and their children live in King's Cross-type bed and breakfast pads. Easy words about racial equality while Asians get excrement pushed through their letter boxes, and sometimes have to go to work in taxi-cabs to avoid assault on housing estates.'

This unmasking of the ideology of our society stands in stark contrast to the lame defences of the Irish Catholic Church's privileges which was the only kind of reply given by Irish churchmen when in debate with Dr O'Brien in the 1970s. Would that many more on this side of the Irish Sea might take Monsignor

Kent's closing words to heart: 'Certainly my gospel makes me impatient and occasionally imprudent. But sometimes it really is folly to be wise.'

EMPOWERING THE PEOPLE

In a paper he was writing at the time of his death in March 1981 Bishop Peter Birch wrote: 'Here in Ireland we have need of some new form of liberation theology, one for ourselves.' Referring to the need to bring the bible alive for people, he wrote: 'If the poor. . . were to read the scriptures in the way suggested, they would become rebels. They would rebel against their own rejection and they would rise up against the waste that is part of modern living. It is out of such rejection that what we call liberation theology has come.' As well as confronting the rich and their view of the world the Church must be helping to make rebels of the poor, helping them to be made powerful by their reading of the bible. For what perpetuates the injustices of our society is the sense of powerlessness among those most directly suffering from them. Up to now the effect of the Church on the poor has been to make them submit to these injustices. It has largely taught them an image of a God who would punish them if they stood up to their oppressors, whether it be a brutal husband, an exploiting landlord or employer, a dismissive civil servant or a patronising priest. This image of God, very far from the God of the bible, would comfort in times of suffering but not empower them to struggle for liberation.

These, then, are the new challenges through which the Church in many parts of the world is beginning to re-discover the power of the gospel to transform both individual lives and social structures. Having made an option for the poor many Church leaders have found, to use their own words, that they have been converted by the poor to really understand the gospel. They refuse to rest content with enunciating general principles on justice and then leaving it up to the politicians and economists to apply these in practice, a neat way through which the Irish bishops constantly opt out of concretely confronting the system of social injustice in Ireland and those who benefit from it. Rather should they make concrete judgements on whole areas of government policy, as the American bishops did in their major pastoral letter on nuclear weapons, and then complement these with actions such as that of Archbishop Hunthausen of Seattle who withheld half his income tax in protest at spending on nuclear weapons or Bishop Murphy of Richmond who refuses to allow the army recruit in the schools of his diocese. Many Latin American episcopacies have used pastoral letters concretely to analyse the effects of capitalism on the poor of their countries and to demand a new popular and socialist economic and political system eradicating dependence on the multi-national companies for development and, instead, mobilising the great wealth and talent of the people themselves. But to do this demands getting close to the people, especially the poor, and seeing how society operates from their standpoint. This is the step that Irish Church leaders have still not taken. In Ireland a Christian response to these new demands has been largely left to small groups of lay people, clergy and religious.

READING

Stanislaus Kennedy, *One Million Poor*. Turoe Press, Dublin, 1981.
Conference on Poverty 1981. The Council for Social Welfare, Dublin, 1982.
Donal Dorr, *Option for the Poor: A Hundred Years of Vatican Social Teaching*. Gill and Macmillan, Dublin, 1983.
Unemployment: Challenge to Christians. Dominican Publications, Dublin, 1983.

8. A New Church for a New Ireland

Ours is not the first generation of Irish people faced with the challenge to fashion a new Church to serve the new needs of a changing society. The last generation of Irish people to face this challenge was growing up just about two hundred years ago, at the end of the eighteenth century. The response of those young Christians was highly creative, fashioning a network of new institutions often in the face of staunch clerical opposition. That many of these new institutions, the male and female religious orders which founded and extended throughout the country a Catholic school and health-care system, have grown even more clericalised and conservative than the clergy themselves, must not lead us to forget that they were all founded by young lay men and women to be lay movements. Without the radical vision and tenacity of these lay people, Nano Nagle, Mary Aikenhead, Catherine McAuley and Edmund Rice, no new model of Church could have developed as successfully as it did in the last century.

Though living in a very different society throwing up very different needs, the challenge for us today is similar. The lessons of the last century teach us that a new model of Church will never emerge from Church leaders but rather from lay people helped by junior clergy who can discern the emerging needs in society and fashion creative responses to them. The challenge to Church leaders is to support such initiatives, discerning those which embody a truly transforming vision for our society derived from the heart of the gospel. All too often, unfortunately, Church leaders seek to defend the old rather than support the emergence of the new.

It is from the Third World today that we see such a new model of Church emerging with greatest clarity. Though it may take different forms in different parts of the world, the similarities of this new model, whether emerging in Latin America, Africa or Asia, are remarkable. Everywhere it is based on a new cell structure, usually called the basic Christian community, where people meet not just for traditional religious services as we know them but to share their lives and their struggles, to deepen their knowledge of the bible and of social injustice, to plan actions together to eradicate those injustices and, from this standpoint, to celebrate the sacraments as a real meeting with the liberating God of the bible.

The fruit of this new model of Church was forcefully expressed in an interview from prison with an Irish Columban priest, Fr Niall O'Brien, charged in the Philippines with the murder of a local mayor. In the interview (*Irish Times,* 14 February 1984), Fr O'Brien said that the charge against him and his fellow eight defendants is 'a calculated plot to silence the voice of a Church that takes the side of the poor and oppressed.' The basic Christian community, he said, 'is based on the principle of sharing everything as equals, with everyone participating in decision-making. The priest is just one member among equals, which promotes a spirit of self-reliance strongly opposed to handouts and charity. However, the Filipino military has classified these communities as "subversive" because they constitute an organised stance for human rights, a challenge to the sugar barons and the property classes and, therefore, a threat to the status-quo.'

Such a new model, therefore, brings the Church back into the centre of people's lives and struggles with consequences that the Church has not had to suffer in a widespread way since the early centuries of its life. In Latin America alone it is estimated that the number of Christians killed, usually with great brutality, over the past twenty years for living out the full consequences of their faith reaches into the tens of thousands while in the same period over a hundred priests have been killed, over one thousand arrested and over three hundred expelled from the countries where they worked. Neither is this new model confined to Third World countries. Throughout Western Europe, North America and even some countries of Eastern Europe networks of basic Christian communities are developing very similar to those in Third World countries.

NEW MODEL OF CHURCH

A new model of Church for our day will, therefore, grow from the people themselves. As society more and more isolates people from one another, breaking down the traditional bonds of the extended family or of the local community, the Church is finding that the parish structure is no longer adequate to create any real community among people. This can happen only where the parish is seen as a community of communities with people creating their primary community on their own streets, meeting in each other's houses. The parish can then take on the functions of providing resources for these smaller communities, everything from simple booklets to running courses in response to community needs. Usually a parish would have a pastoral team of priests, sisters and lay people accompanying the communities in growing to maturity. Meanwhile within each of the smaller communities the people would be sharing in ever-deeper ways together, deepening their knowledge of the bible and of the structures of injustice in society, attacking this injustice in ways that could vary from leading protest marches to setting up a co-operative and celebrating their lives in weekly liturgies planned and run by themselves. The parish church can then be used for the liturgy on some of the Church's major feasts to symbolise the communities' links with the wider Church. Far from making the priest redundant, as some might fear, this new model frees the priest from much of the administrative chores with which he is presently burdened for a ministry that can concentrate much more centrally on building up the people in the faith. As Fr Niall O'Brien ended his article in *The Furrow* in February 1984 on his six year experiment in building basic Christian communities: 'I recommend to any priest who feels his vocation to be a bit pointless – go to a very poor place and throw yourself into the work of starting small Christian communities. Don't do it on your own. Do it with others. I hope your experiment will be as happy as mine.'

If the basic community is truly the cell of a new Church, it will have to relate to the wider Church around it. This can often lead to tensions and problems where parishes organised in basic communities live alongside traditional parishes. This poses a challenge for the diocese if it is to share the commitment to building a new model of Church. Many Third World dioceses have responded to this challenge by initiating a process of pastoral planning, bringing representatives of each of the communities in the diocese together with representatives of the priests and with the bishop to reflect on the needs of the people and how to respond to them as Church. This will usually involve a thorough political, social, economic and cultural analysis of the area where the diocese is in order to identify concretely who are the rich and who the poor, and in what ways are the poor being exploited. Then out of this analysis is made the choice of pastoral options for the following years. Typically such options will involve building basic communities, supporting workers' struggles, defending human rights. A detailed plan will then be drawn up outlining how these options can be implemented in practice. At all stages of this process, from drawing up the plan to implementing it and later evaluating it and learning from its successes and failures in order to develop even further, ordinary lay people will be involved on a completely equal level with the priest and the bishop. In Ireland today it is not difficult to see how such a process might lead the Church to make options to side with the unemployed or small farmers, to expose the structures of injustice in our society, or to take up the issue of inadequate housing and exploitative landlords.

For a Church like the Irish Catholic Church, with a highly developed network of schools, hospitals and other social services, this process poses a particular challenge. How can schools run by religious orders and serving the privileged elite in our society be transformed to empower the poor? How can a health-care system which all too often accepts the forms of drug-dependent medicine propagated by the multi-national drug companies be transformed into centres where people can be educated in simple ways in preventive medicine and in the social causes of so much of our illnesses? For too long Catholic schools and hospitals have simply provided a parallel for Catholics to the structure being provided by the state for others though in Ireland the Catholic system *became* the state system almost completely. The challenge now is not to give over all Catholic institutions to the state, though that will have to happen in many cases, but to create a Catholic system of education and health-care which is truly an alternative, not just serving the poor and oppressed but empowering them in such a way that they can cease being victims of an unjust society and become the creators of a new society of justice. Again, in this, the example of the new forms of education for social awareness, or conscientisation as it is usually called, and the new forms of community-based health-care, being pioneered by the Church in many parts of the Third World hold many very important lessons for us.

SEEDS OF CHANGE

Already one can discern in Ireland the seeds of such a newChurch just beginning to emerge. This is most evident in the new consciousness to be found among the Christians who attend local adult education courses or discussion groups up and down the country. No longer are many of them attending to be educated in Church teaching, but far more they are beginning to express their demand to be helped to create a new model ofChurch which could relate to their lives and concerns. Often great anger and frustration is expressed at the mediocrity of the institutional Church and its complacency not just about the growing crisis of faith but also the growing levels of injustice in Irish society. This indicates a major potential for the growth of a new model of Church which is only in isolated cases being adequately channelled into ways that can help it grow and find expression.

Where it has been channelled the results have been impressive. A number of parishes, particularly in Dublin, have facilitated the growth of basic Christian communities. The parish of Dun Laoghaire is the most notable example where the parish priest, Fr Chris Mangan, translated with impressive success the experience he had gained from working in Chile. Elsewhere small groups are being facilitated to discover how reading the bible relates to their struggles for justice. Fr Ciaran Earley, OMI, who worked in Brazil, has written a simple booklet called *The Struggle to be God's People* outlining a series of steps he has used with various groups in Dublin's inner city. Another factor facilitating the growth of basic communities is the move by many groups of priests and sisters to live in deprived areas among the people. Sharing the people's life experience at close quarters, these groups are searching for more adequate pastoral responses to the people's needs, often having to resist strong pressure from the people themselves to fit into the traditional clerical or religious roles. Such a process is bound to bear more fruit in years to come.

Numerous Christian youth groups are emerging seeking to take as a priority the demands of justice. To help these groups reflect together the Young Christian Workers and the Student Christian Movement have organised meetings at which representatives of such groups can develop their awareness and share their forms of response. Such meetings have brought together groups as diverse as the St Vincent de Paul Society and Christians for Socialism or the Laurentian Society from Trinity College, Dublin, and the People's Mass group from Ballymun. From an initiative of the Young Christian Workers a new quarterly magazine called *Resource* has developed which, as its name implies, provides individuals and groups with resources to reflect on areas of injustice in Irish and international life, on capitalism and socialism, on papal social teaching, on spirituality for struggle and on the lessons to be learned from what different groups are doing to combat injustice. Action from Ireland (AFrI), a small group which seeks to draw the links between the arms race, injustice in the Third World and injustice at home, has begun to re-interpret traditional Irish spirituality by sending a Brigid's Cross to each of the world's leaders reminding them of the lesson of Brigid who sold her father's best sword to feed a poor man. Among other groups in the Church, also, much work is being done to develop an awareness of the causes of injustice and to stimulate more adequate pastoral responses. Numerous religious orders, particularly female ones, have spent weekends going through a process of social analysis. As a result of this many are painfully trying to adapt their ministries, finding in the process that the institutions they inherited from their predecessors act as a major inhibiting factor for them. A Sisters for Justice group has been meeting for a number of years mobilising sisters to get involved in struggling against concrete cases of injustice.

The fundamental objective of all these groups and initiatives is the development of a new model of Church empowering the people to discover their faith as a resource for building a new society of justice. Such an objective has also begun to break through at leadership level in the Church. This happened in a dramatic way at the tenth anniversary celebrations of *Trocaire* in June 1983 in Galway when the calls by prominent Third World speakers for a Church allied to the cause of the poor found echo when a leader of the travellers, Ms Nan Joyce, made a public plea for a '*Trocaire* for travellers'. Many of the 350 Irish delegates present sympathised with the often-expressed view that there was a major contradiction between the Irish Church's effective concern for injustice and its victims abroad while its activities served by and large to perpetuate a society of injustice at home. The theme chosen by the National Conference of Priests of Ireland for their 1983 annual meeting was unemployment and the closing statement of that meeting marked a new breakthrough for a document coming from Church leaders in Ireland in that it sought to identify with the unemployed whom it called 'the new oppressed in our society' rather than just offering to help them. 'We want to stand with you in your struggle,' the priests said and pledged themselves to 'specific action', such as helping redundant workers establish co-operatives and using their resources to set up local development committees. Even if a tiny percentage of the priests of Ireland took this new stress seriously it could transform their understanding of their ministry.

What is still lacking, however, is a more coherent pastoral strategy from Church leaders to foster basic communities and initiate a genuine process of pastoral planning, facilitating ordinary people to express their needs and develop a plan to guide the growth of a new model of Church. Without this the danger is that these initiatives will remain isolated and that the Church will continue to be trapped within its traditional institutions and styles of ministry. As yet there are very few signs that Irish Church leaders trust lay people enough to welcome a real expression of their needs or to allow them a central role in fashioning a pastoral plan for the future. Yet unless this happens it is more than likely that the great potential of generosity and goodwill towards the Church felt by many will evaporate into cynicism and hostility. Already this process is more advanced than most Church leaders may care to acknowledge.

AN ACCOUNT OF HOPE

'Give an account of the hope that is within you,' St Peter wrote in his first letter (3:15). Many people in the western world find such an account impossible to give, fearful as they are of annihilation through nuclear war or of the growing injustices and inequality which characterise world society. Many live quite hopeless and despairing lives.

Central to Christian faith, however, is the vision of 'a new heavens and a new earth, the home of justice' (2 Peter 3-13). Though awareness of our social situation quickly kills any easy optimism about creating a new society of justice, any form of Christian faith which does not hunger and thirst for justice is false faith. But what real hope is there that the Irish Catholic Church could become a social movement characterised by its commitment to justice? What hope is there for the creation of a new model of Church? Certainly the signs that such might happen are meagre indeed. But belief in the God of the bible is belief in a God who is making all things new. The whole of the history of the Church from the time of Jesus is a history of decay and rejuvenation. If Jesus himself preached a message of life and of justice then the Church has again and again had to have its complicity in injustice severely confronted by the new movements of growth and renewal which have emerged at various times during its history. Whether it was the Franciscans and Dominicans breaking free from the wealth and rigidity of monasticism in the 1200s, the Jesuits introducing a new flexibility and discipline needed after the reformation in the 1500s, St Vincent de Paul founding the Daughters of Charity as a group of laywomen dedicated to serving the poor rather than living enclosed lives in the 1600s, or the various teaching orders of the last century bringing the Church back into some areas of public life after the trauma of the French revolution and its consequences, the Church has been challenged again and again to be faithful to the life-giving message of Jesus. Each of these movements of renewal has involved creating new communities to embody the message of Jesus in fresh ways and also involved moving more closely in touch with the poor again. The central emphasis on community and the poor characterise the new movement which is renewing the Church today. But, as happened at every other time of renewal in history, these are understood today in new ways. So the communities emerging now are not new religious orders of celibates but mixed communities of lay men and women, married and single. The ways these are touching the world of the poor in our day is not through providing services for them but through empowering them to break out of their powerlessness. The Church is becoming not just a Church for the poor but a 'Church of the poor', to use a phrase of Pope John Paul.

The hope that a new model of Church might emerge in Ireland, therefore, is based on the fact that only such a Church could be fully faithful to the message of Jesus and to the lessons of Church history. When John the Baptist sent his disciples to ask Jesus if he was the Messiah or were they to look for another (Luke 7:18-23), Jesus did not answer with a theological treatise but pointed to the result of his work: 'The blind see again, the lame walk, lepers are cleansed, and the deaf hear, the dead are raised to life and the Good News is proclaimed to the poor.' Only when it is obvious to all in Irish society that the Church is raising up those deadened by the inhuman cycle of consumerism and manipulation by hidden vested interests, that it is opening the eyes of those blinded by the lies of advertising and the false world created by the media and that it is proclaiming a good news of liberation to that thirty per cent of our people who lack the basic material or cultural necessities of life, can we say that it is following the example of Jesus.

Embodying such a vision will demand a painful transformation for most Irish Christians both in the ways that they understand their faith and in the structures through which they live it out. But for those who believe that the gospel of Jesus Christ should be a saving force in Irish society nothing less is adequate. There is much evidence to suggest that for unemployed, deprived young people at the moment the main saving force they can identify is Provisional Sinn Féin. Condemnations by Christians, no matter how eloquent, can do little to change such perceptions. There is no substitute for determined and radical action by groups of committed Christians.

READING

James O'Halloran, *Living Cells: Developing Small Christian Community*. Dominican Publications, Dublin, and Orbis Books, New York, 1984.

Ciaran Earley, *The Struggle to be God's People*. The Irish Commission for Justice and Peace, Dublin, 1984.